HELP YOUR CHILD
WITH READING

HELP YOUR CHILD WITH READING

by Wendy Body

with contributions from Julie Garnett, Pam Fudge, Wendy McCracken and Daphne Ashton

BBC BOOKS

PHOTO CREDITS

Daphne Ashton pages 10 & 20;
Lupe Cunha Photography pages 14, 31, 40, 53, 66 & 110;
Sally & Richard Greenhill pages 28, 29, 54 & 58;
Camilla Jessel page 21;
Julian Selmes pages 91 & 116;
John Walmsley pages 63 & 96;
Janine Wiedel pages 33 & 131;
Karen Willie pages 25 & 30;
Zefa Picture Library pages 35 & 94.

front cover Image Bank (Claus Dieter Geissler)
back cover Camilla Jessel (both)

Book covers and the illustration on page 60 are reproduced by kind permission
of the publishers.

This book accompanies the BBC TV series
Help your child with reading. *The series was
produced by Jenny Stevens, and prepared in
consultation with the Continuing Education Advisory Council.*

*Published by BBC Books,
a division of BBC Enterprises Limited,
Woodlands, 80 Wood Lane, London W12 0TT
First published 1990
© Wendy Body and Julie Garnett 1990
ISBN 0 563 21543 7
Designed by Trevor & Jacqui Vincent
Illustrations by Kate Simunek
Set in 10/12pt Century Schoolbook
Printed and bound in Great Britain by
Butler & Tanner Ltd, Frome and London
Cover printed by Clays Ltd, St. Ives plc*

CONTENTS

INTRODUCTION   7

Part 1: Getting readyfor reading: 11

ages 0–4
Talk: building the foundations for reading   12
Activities and games for early learning   25
Introducing the world of books   42

Part 2: Starting to read: 54

ages 5–7
Reading in school   55
Sharing books and listening to children reading   67
Games and activities for language development,
      reading and writing   71
Learning about letters   76
Books for beginner readers: ages 5–7   82

Part 3: Moving on with reading: 89

ages 7+
What you can do to encourage the reading habit   90
Reading in the junior school   92
Monitoring your child's progress   98
Books for readers on the move: ages 7+   100
Children with special needs: 108
      Reading problems   108
      Spelling problems   118
      Physical problems   121
      Books for children with special needs   132

Further reading and useful addresses   139
Some typical questions parents ask   141
Index   143

INTRODUCTION

Help your child with reading is the book which accompanies the BBC Television series of that name and which was written while the TV series was being planned. The two have much in common but in a book we are able to provide much more detail and lots of specific suggestions as to how you can best support your child. All parents are keen for their child to learn to read and, as its title suggests, this book is intended to help you to help your child – whether your child is in the process of learning to read at school or whether you want to know how and when to start, even if your child is still a baby.

For convenience, the book is arranged into sections:
Part 1: Getting ready for reading: ages 0–4
Part 2: Starting to read: ages 5–7
Part 3: Moving on with reading: ages 7+ (This third section also contains information about children with special needs.)

It must be stressed, however, that these are only *approximate* age guides. Your child is unique, and so is every other child. Children *do* develop at different rates. Whether it concerns teeth, potty training, first words or learning to read, children will develop at their own pace and forcing or hurrying them along is not to be recommended if you want to have a secure and happy child! Please then, don't look at any one section and dismiss it because you think it is for four-year-olds and your child is five!

One of the best things to have happened in schools during the last few years is the growing awareness of the important role parents can have in supporting their child's learning. Increasingly, it is recognised just how much parents can contribute to and affect their children's learning and progress.

Children spend a large proportion of their time at school and, in the capable hands of their teachers, learn a great deal. But it is you, as a parent, who is your child's first and most important teacher. At school, a child's teacher changes from year to year but you are constant and you can offer so much with regard to supporting your child. Most parents and teachers would agree that the skills of reading are one of the most important things a child has to learn. Many parents want to help but they are not sure of what to do or they worry that they may be doing the wrong thing. This book will help you and, I hope, make it a rewarding experience for you and your child.

For the sake of convenience we have used 'he' throughout the book but, of course, everything is intended for both girls and boys.

Four authors apart from myself have been involved in writing this book. We are all trained teachers and most of us have children of our own.

DAPHNE ASHTON has written the section on talk and children's language development. Daphne works as Senior Portage Pre-school Home Teacher in the County of Avon where her job involves working with parents. She has a speech and language diploma from the University of Reading. She is also a qualified teacher of the hearing impaired and has worked with children in schools and special units.

PAM FUDGE wrote the sections on games and activities for early learning and language development. Pam is the Area Tutor, North Bristol in Avon's Service For Special Educational Needs. She works with children who need support with reading and writing but her job largely involves providing advice and support to teachers.

JULIE GARNETT compiled the four sections on books. She too works in Avon's SSEN and is the Area Tutor for Bath and Wansdyke. She works in schools but much of her time is spent providing in-service education for teachers on reading and language teaching. Julie is also an educational author who has contributed to series for use in schools such as *Reading World* (Longman) and *Sharp-Eye* (Ginn).

WENDY McCRACKEN contributed to the section on children with special educational needs, writing the part about children with sensory and other handicaps. She is a qualified teacher of the deaf and a qualified audiologist. She has recently written a book for parents of deaf children called *Deaf-ability, a resource book for parents of hearing-impaired children* (Multilingual Matters). Wendy lives in Cheshire.

And me? Well, I'm now a Literacy and Language Consultant. I was involved in running Bristol Reading Centre before I gave up my job to concentrate on writing and lecturing. My time is mainly spent running courses for teachers, lecturing throughout the UK, doing talks for parents and writing books. I am the author or editor of over 200 books for children, teachers and parents.

We enjoyed writing this book – we hope you will enjoy reading it!

WENDY BODY
March 1990

Playing with babies builds
the foundations for
learning to talk.

1 GETTING READY FOR READING:
ages 0–4

A large amount of this section is devoted to talk: how children's language develops in the early years and how you can encourage your child with these developing skills. You may think it strange that a book about reading should have so much about talk in it! The reason for this is that the spoken word and learning to talk provide the foundations for the written word and learning to read.

In learning to talk a child is learning about language – the way it is constructed, its patterns, the way words work together to create meaning. This knowledge and understanding about the way language works form the first important steps on the road to becoming a reader. Sharing books with your child takes him or her a little further along that road. Sharing books helps children:

- to appreciate that reading is a pleasurable and satisfying activity which engages the interests and the emotions
- to understand that there is a 'message' or story in print
- to learn about the directional nature of print: left to right along a line; top to bottom of a page; through a book. (You show your child this directional nature of print every time you run your finger under a line of print as you read it.)
- to begin to appreciate that story language can be different from everyday language
- to begin to recognise words/phrases within a familiar context – the story that is read often or the repeating phrases within a story
- to begin to learn that words are made up of letters and that it is the words which tell you what to say and not the pictures, although they are part of the story as a whole.

Children also need to be helped with the beginnings of writing. They need encouragement to experiment with scribbling and drawing to help them learn pencil control. This is touched on in this section but you will find more information in Part 2.

TALK: BUILDING THE FOUNDATIONS FOR READING

You and your home are the centre of your child's world and you are his natural teacher. You are with him from his birth and you both learn about each other as you live together. From the moment he is born, he is aware of your individual smell, your eyes, your voice and how you handle him. Cash in on this initial awareness of you – it can be a satisfying, enjoyable beginning to your long-term relationship.

A simple outline and description of the development of talk: 0–2 years

In the first months of life a baby's basic needs are met through the cries of hunger, pain, pleasure, boredom or discomfort. Then at 3–6 months cooing and smiling to another person, or just to himself, develops to more easily recognised sounds of babbling. These are experiments with sound and pitch. They are not yet the beginnings of words.

When a baby is about twelve months old, excited, proud parents often shout 'He's said his first word!', as he looks at his father (or any male!) and says 'dada'. Parents interpret this as a first word when, in actual fact, it is really highlighting how clever parents are to recognise those sounds as a possible word. It is their excited response that makes the sound important to the child. He continues to shape his sounds into recognisable words through experiment and trial-and-error until, within three and a half years, he has achieved sentences. It becomes an exciting game – a fascinating enjoyable game for everyone involved as words are recognised. It is also vitally important. We need words throughout life to:

- communicate our thoughts, feelings and ideas
- co-operate with others
- be confident in the world around us.

9–18 months

The baby may be using single words – 'dada/dere/no/more' etc in a meaningful way.

18 months – 2 years

Two words are being linked together – 'dada dere/gone car' etc but the order of the words may still vary. Listen out for extras like:

    'dada going' ('ing' on the end of the verb)

    'socks/shoes' ('s' added to make plurals of words)

    'teddy walked' (added 'ed' to the end of the verb for past tense)

Talking to your child and encouraging language development

0–1 year

Try to keep eye contact as you talk to him while he lies in your arms or is having his nappy changed. Of course he doesn't understand what you are saying to him but talk to him as if he does. Just as you enjoy talking to your baby, so he will enjoy listening to and looking for the sound of your voice. As you smile, talk and move your head, listen to your own voice and you'll notice how it changes and softens; it's probably more soothing and more sing-song than usual and your baby responds to this pleasant, calming tone of voice. Nodding and moving your head from side to side or up and down encourages him to follow with his eyes and to listen. Try to vary the tone of your voice as much as you can – you can even sing your 'conversations' sometimes. Some parents feel silly about talking to new-born babies in this way; there's no need to feel embarrassed – what you are doing is taking the first steps towards teaching your baby to talk!

How calm you are and how much you smile can affect your handling of the baby. Very firm handling is often accompanied by a serious voice and an unsmiling face; it can result in a tense and unhappy baby. Relaxed handling affects both the baby and the parent and builds up mutual confidence. Babies need to be touched when we talk to them. Touching is very important and often neglected; we can express our feelings through touch when we cannot find the right words. When babies are distressed we stroke them to calm them; we smile and stroke their faces when they are smiling. This pleases or

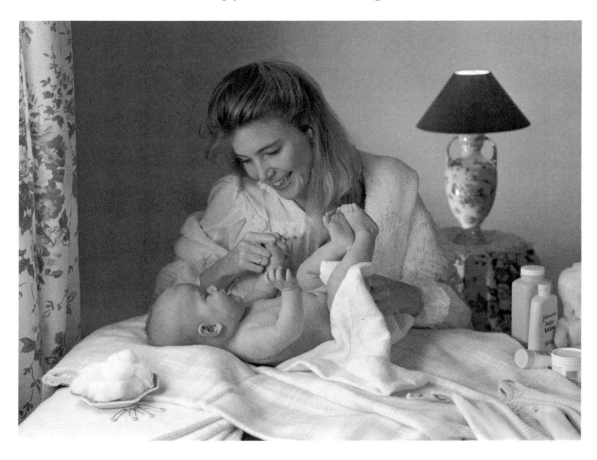

Opportunities for 'conversations' with your baby arise during any part of the daily routine.

comforts and answers immediate needs as well as acting as an expression of our feelings. We are 'talking' together through touch. These early responses to what a parent is doing quickly progress to a smile and the first cooing sounds at about five or six weeks. Encourage this by responding back to him with smiles and noises like his own. At about this age a baby will smile or stop crying when he sees or hears a member of the family. He waits to be picked up, he turns to look at a familiar face, he is listening and reacting. Try starting a 'conversation' by using sounds he often makes and wait to see if he echoes you, or smiles and waits for you to do it again. Introduce new noises and sounds – blow 'raspberries', burble at him with your lips, or make sounds with your tongue like a cat lapping!

Tickling your baby will make him smile and encourage him to gurgle. If you also say something like 'Do you like that then?' as you smile at him you are encouraging him to listen to your voice as well as his own gurgles and chuckles. He is becoming aware that if you do something he can respond and vice versa. This is important because he is also learning about taking turns, which is what proper conversations require.

Once he is aware of his own varying sounds, a baby begins to experiment with his voice; he loves you to join in by making him laugh, chuckle or squeal. Once he is aware of the 'tunes' he can make with his own voice, a baby will imitate the voice patterns you make. For example, if you start in a high 'OOoo' with your voice coming down, he may try to copy you. He will also imitate you in clapping hands or waving 'bye-bye'.

By listening to the 'tunes' of your voice your baby is also becoming aware of your moods. A happy 'tune' when you are smiling is very different from a rising 'no . . .' and a serious face if he is doing wrong. By the age of one he responds by stopping what he is doing and looking tearful or forlorn. Your tone of voice is making him wary and he is learning that life is not all smiles!

1–2 years

We normally reinforce our speech with gestures to help a child's understanding; if, for example, he is touching something precious, you respond with 'No!' in a stern voice, plus a warning finger. Your voice, gesture and look all help him to 'read' the message correctly and act accordingly!

Babies need to explore a wider world with you whenever possible instead of being in one room for most of the day. Try to take him with you when you are making beds, in the kitchen or out in the garden so that he can, within reason, explore and handle things. Talk about what you are doing and let him join in: say 'Pull the sheet' when standing against the bed or 'Put them in here' as you load the washing machine together, for example. At such times it is best not to make your sentences too long. He is expecting you to understand him and he is trying to understand you so too many words can be confusing.

Children need to be praised when they carry out simple instructions successfully and you can respond to his action with additional words eg 'Good boy, now shut the door.' It is also a good idea to use similar patterns of words for what you do each day: 'Shoes on/ coat on/ in the buggy/ in the car' etc.

Anything can happen around the two-year-old stage and shyness, anxiety and temper tantrums are common. It can help if you encourage your child to get to know other people outside the family eg next door, at the shops and at toddler groups. Try including him in your conversations with others eg 'Show Mrs Jones your red shoes' or 'Wave bye-bye to the lady' when you leave shops, the health centre etc. By gradually involving him with others while you are still there, his confidence will grow as his experience of people talking to him extends from day to day.

A simple outline and description of the development of talk: 2–4 years

2–2½ years

By now, children are using three words together to form simple sentences eg 'dada go car'. Your child may well continue to leave out little words ('go sleep' instead of 'go to sleep'). This is because he is not yet aware of them.

Listen out for your child beginning to use pronouns and encourage the use of words like: *my* teddy; *your* car; *his* mummy; *our* house; *her* dog.

2½–3 years

Gradually, children begin to use four or more words in a sentence: 'Me going to town today.' The use of question words and commands are beginning too: 'Where my mummy gone?' 'Give my teddy (to) me.' Children will also be starting to link words with 'and' at this age: 'Me and mummy'.

3–3½ years

By now you will notice your child using longer sentences which are linked by 'and': 'Daddy digged in the garden and he felled over and he dirty and my mummy laughed.' Other linking words may also be beginning to emerge – the use of 'but/so/'cos'. At this age a child has learned many ways of using simple sentences; once he discovers the word 'and' his sentences can go on for ever! He has now learned to create language but he is still some way from adult speech. He will be eight or nine before he can really understand and use the more complicated structures successfully.

$3\frac{1}{2}$–4 years

You will notice your child making mistakes. This is perfectly normal and should be expected. It demonstrates that he is working out and experimenting with the rules of language for himself. In learning to cope with the regularities and irregularities of language, children commonly say things like: 'him going now', 'you bettern't do that' or 'nobody don't like me'.

Children don't learn to talk simply by imitating adults. If they did, they wouldn't make such mistakes as 'mouses' instead of 'mice'. Having learned 'walk, walked' or 'jump, jumped' it is perfectly logical for them to say 'I goed'! 'I went for a walk' takes a lot of thought!

If children learned through imitation only, they would use baby-talk. Listen to adults talking to a baby – they often use a sing-song voice: 'Who's a bootiful boy den?' You don't hear a twelve-month-old baby use that pattern of voice, however! Imitation does play a part, though, in learning how to pronounce words. As adults we often hear someone speaking and think to ourselves: 'Oh, *that's* how you say that word!'

Talking to your child and encouraging language development

By this age a child needs as much independence as possible while he explores and plays – not least of all because this encourages him to comment, ask questions and report back: 'Me do it', 'what Thomas doing?', 'sheep goed there' etc. Young children need to mix and play with others of a similar age. Once you have a child, it is usually easy to meet other families and opportunities arise for joint play while you are there with him. When you join in yourself he is learning to share you as well as to share playthings.

Children love having adult clothes to pretend in: to be you, grandad, the playgroup leader and so on. Being 'someone else' known to them can produce some interesting 'different voices' eg soft, gruff or loud. When adults join in with children's pretence *everyone* has fun and enjoyment!

It is important to try and set aside special times when you can really talk to each other – even if this is only for a few minutes a day when nothing else is going on. This might be when other members of the family have left each morning. Talk about what you plan to do that day: 'We'll make the beds. Then go shopping. We need bread and coffee – you tell mummy.' He might say, 'And go school.' Try to build on what he says by adding a few words like: 'Yes, we're going to school after dinner.'

Depending on the way it is used, television can help children's language development as well as offering more general learning and entertainment. Children's programmes and videos can provide you with special time together if you are able to take the opportunity to enjoy programmes *with* your child. Comment together on what you see: 'Oh, look at Tom, isn't he naughty?' 'Hide Jerry!' 'Here's Thomas!' 'What's he doing?' 'He's happy, isn't he?' Talk back to the characters (even if you, as an adult, feel a bit daft about doing it, your child won't!) and recall what happened before as well as inviting your child to talk about the programme after it is over. It's obviously very tempting for busy parents to let children watch TV by themselves while the adult gets on with something else. Joining in the viewing together, however, is not only educationally important, it's also fun and gives you a break too!

By three years old, children love stories, nursery rhymes and action jingles and will demand their favourites time and time again. Try to make it obvious to your child that you really enjoy these sharing times too (even if it *is* the ninety-ninth time you've recited 'Humpty Dumpty'!). That way you show him that these are important activities. You can also tell him any favourite stories or family episodes you remember and then celebrate afterwards with 'That was good wasn't it? Shall we have a drink and a biscuit now?' It all adds to making it special!

Books help children develop their language too!

Books offer yet another golden opportunity to have special times with your child. Sharing books gives such pleasure to both parent and child – especially pre-schoolers because their early handling of books can lead to life-long pleasure. Looking at books together means the child having the parent's complete attention, probably by sitting on a lap, secure and happy.

At six months a baby can hold a straight-edged, flat, light object, so why shouldn't he hold a small cardboard book? 'Look, it's a book' you can say as you help him to hold it. At this age he is able to look at pictures for a few seconds too. Try finding a simple picture of a brightly coloured ball. Hold his hand, point to the picture together and go round and round, saying: 'Look . . . ball!'

At 9–12 months a baby can use his finger and thumb to pick up a sweet so why not use a finger and thumb to turn a page? Lift it at the corner, saying as you hold his hand: 'Turn the page . . . good boy.' In these ways you are introducing the important ideas of 'book' and 'page' in his first year.

At 15 months a baby can look at coloured pictures in books with real interest. It is important to try and find books with simple pictures or photographs – not fussy, busy ones like cartoons at this stage. The baby will begin to find his favourite pictures and may even point with a forefinger.

At 2–3 years a child can turn pages singly using finger and thumb himself and can identify family members in photographs. You could try making your child his own book with photos of himself and the family. Talk about it and write simple two- or three-word explanations under each picture eg Sarah's blue bike.

The sort of published books you can use at this stage are:
- cardboard beginner books with two or three words on a page
- 'Find-the-animal' books where the same animal hides on each page for the child to find and point to
- books which ask a simple question eg 'Can you jump?' These encourage the child to answer 'Yes/Yes I can'
- stories with repetition where the child can join in
- colourful 'Look-and-find' books where the child is encouraged to find and name objects in scenes.

(See pages 44–52 for a detailed list of books to use with young children.)

Such books introduce children to 'book language' from an early age and the closer it matches their own understanding the easier it is for them. Why are certain books favourites? Is it the size? The shape? The colour? The smell? The smooth feel? The content? One thing is for sure, once a child has discovered his favourites he will sit and play happily with them, turning the pages and hardly ever with the book upside down.

Children seem to react differently to books. One child will turn to his favourite pages, point and talk to himself as he looks at the pictures. Adults can be pushed away if they interrupt and the child may say: 'No – mine!' Another child will start at the beginning and turn the pages methodically and carefully until the end of the story, just looking and passing on. Such activities can continue for a surprisingly long time – sometimes longer than with any toy. What have children like this understood from looking at their books? It doesn't matter as long as the very young child is enjoying himself and so learning that books are friends!

Close to dad and close to a book!

Books can have a settling and calming effect on children and can be a godsend when dealing with a tired, over-excited or poorly young child. This is one of the reasons for the traditional bedtime story. It settles a child to sleep and it is also another opportunity to share special time together.

It's very important, though, to include books in your child's daytime play activities. Keep some books near his toys so that he can turn to them for himself. Help your child to learn careful handling of books but try not to make them so precious that he is frightened to touch them!

This section of the book is about talk and building the foundations for reading. When we look at books with children we normally comment and ask lots of questions. Let's look at how the ability to use questions develops in young children – not least of all because it reminds us not to make our own

It's never too soon to get used to books....

questions too complicated! There are three main ways of asking questions:

- we may just ask something in a questioning tone, ie your voice goes up as you ask: 'You're going?'
- change the word order and 'you are going' becomes 'Are you going?'
- we add a question word – how, when, why, where and so on.

At 12 months

A baby can question with a rising tone of voice 'dada?' meaning 'where's daddy?'

At 18 months

'What dat?' or 'Where dada?' show that the question word is beginning to be used.

At 2 years

'Mummy gone' becomes 'Where Mummy gone?' Children have not yet learned to change the word order to form a question.

At 2½–3 years

A child may ask a question in two ways: when he says 'Are you coming?' he is changing the word order and when he says 'Where you are coming?' he is trying to tackle the word order *and* trying to make it a question at the same time! No wonder it has been said that it is the eighth wonder of the world that a child ever learns language successfully!

Parents seem naturally able to adapt their questions to the needs of their child as in the following examples:

2-year-old child: 'Daddy gone?'
Parent: 'Yes, Daddy's gone. He's gone to work, hasn't he?'
The parent makes the same point in a similar way but adds to it.
3-year-old child (playing with farm animals): 'Me want pig now. In there.'
Parent: 'You want a pig? This one? Or that one?'
Child: 'Dat pink pig. In there.'
Parent: 'The little pink pig? He lives in a sty, doesn't he?'

This kind of exchange has several important functions to notice. By repeating or echoing what the child says, the parent checks that what the child says is what the parent thought it was. It also gives the child the chance to correct any misunderstanding. By adding the remark about the sty the parent is demonstrating how adding extra information keeps a conversation going and makes it interesting. The parent's encouragement and sentence pattern helps the child to practise and polish what he says. He's talking and he's learning. What he experiences at home can decide and influence a child's attitude to learning when he goes to school.

Acquiring sounds in speech

Children do not master sounds in a strict order, but they generally develop in something like the following way:

First   p b t d m n w
Second   g k ng (as in sing) h
Third   s f l y (as in you)
Fourth   ch (as in chip) sh (as in shoe)
Fifth   j (as in juice) v z r
Sixth   th (as in this) th (as in thin) shj (as in measure)

Individual children may find difficulty with any sound. It can depend if it is at the beginning, middle or end of a word: eg 'b' is said correctly in bin/robin, but 'disturv' is said for 'disturb'. Children also vary in how long it can take them to master a sound. A child may say 'shoe', then it can become 'soo', change to 'doo' and eventually establish itself as 'shoe'.

Some seven-year-olds can still have trouble with the sound 'th'. 'This feather' is frequently said as 'dis fever' or 'vis fever' and 'think' often turns into 'fink'; 'Three trees' can be 'tree trees'. If one questions the child by asking 'tree trees?', a child can correct it very strongly by saying 'No, tree trees'. A young child realises when an adult is saying it wrongly, but not when he is saying it wrongly himself.

Most of the child's sound system has been acquired by the age of five years. Some take longer, so do be patient before you worry about any need for speech therapy. The most difficult sound groups to acquire are triple combinations, eg 'str' as in 'strength', which can be 'stwenf/stwenth/strenth'. A similar word is 'twelfths' (lfths), frequently said as 'twefs/twelfs/twelths'.

All these approximations given as examples have been recorded from both children and adults!

Early language comes from handling and doing things

Suggested infant activities to encourage:

eye movements	Dangle a ball on a string.
head and eye turning	Hang tinfoil strands to catch light, shake a rattle, small bell etc.
holding (either hand)	Adult's finger then rattles, spoons, bricks etc. Vary weight, shapes, sizes.
use of finger and thumb	Large crumb, small sweet, coin in money box.
watching a face	Baby mirror to see himself.
reaching	Sound-making toys on strings.

Once a child can sit up and hold a variety of small objects, introduce him to word-directed activities. (Some examples are listed below.) He may not be able to understand all the words at first, but the activities help him to develop that understanding and eventually use the words.

stacking bricks	'on there'
posting boxes	'in there'
pretend play with everyday objects	
cup/brush/etc	'Teddy drink'/'brush hair'/etc
objects in containers	'put it in'/'take it out'/'in and out'
toys that build up/ knock down	'up'/'down'/'more'/'all gone'
beginner puzzles	'in there'/'by that one'/'turn it round'
pairs games (eg Spot)	'find another the same'
dressing up clothes	hat/shoes/coat etc 'Mummy's hat'/'Daddy's shoes'/'big coat' etc
doll's clothes	'put dolly's hat on'/'arms in'/'legs in'/'over her head' etc
books	'hold the book'/'turn the page'/'turn over'/'see the . . .'/'find the . . .'/'show me . . .'/'where's the . . .'/'tell me about . . .'/'what's happened?' etc.

ACTIVITIES AND GAMES FOR EARLY LEARNING

Working out what you want to achieve

A question asked by most parents is 'How can I be sure that I'm giving my child the best opportunities?' As a new parent you may find yourself either at the receiving end of a wealth of good advice, which can be confusing, or at a loss for advice when you need it.

If we start with the idea that we learn from our experiences and actions, it follows that our children need to interact with their world in order to learn.

Your child

Anything can fascinate a baby!

Your child has a natural curiosity and a need to learn about his world. He will do this with confidence, by experimenting.

You as parent or carer

You have your love and instinct to protect and care for your child. This includes being his teacher. Take a lesson from your child: have confidence in yourself and experiment. Common sense is useful to fall back on when you wonder if you're doing the right thing. Providing you and your child are enjoying yourselves, your experiences together can only be of value. One of the most important things you can offer your child is your time: time to communicate and enjoy yourselves.

Playthings in the home

Your own environment provides an endless source of ideas and activities for early learning. It's very easy to be tempted to spend a great deal of money buying all sorts of toys and games for your child but this is not always necessary. As a general rule, it is best to think about what your child is likely to do with the toy and then consider what he will gain from playing with it. It's quite often the packaging that is enjoyed more! You will find that there are quite a few things around your home that can be enjoyed just as much as shop-bought toys. If you have the time, there are also things that can be made quickly and cheaply.

The first few months before your baby is able to move himself around

For your child to understand his world he needs to have freedom to:

See and watch

Give him lots of opportunity to see different things. When awake, place him where he can watch you or whatever is going on around. Colourful pictures, toys and a mobile will draw his attention. (See page 36.)

Listen and make sounds

Watch for when he begins to link sounds with actions. Call your baby from different positions so he has to look up, down or to either side to see you.

Learn to get on with others

Talk to him and listen to the sounds he tries out himself. Songs and rhymes will catch his attention. He will listen to all the different sounds around him. Try playing different types of music.

Play

He will begin to respond with smiles, noises and touching. Keep responding and you will find that you begin to take turns.

Taste and smell

Do not forget that as well as different tastes, your baby will experience the different smells around him, eg in the kitchen, bath, garden.

Feel, touch and grasp

Give him objects made of different materials – eg woolly, furry, spongy or smooth – to reach out for and touch. If you are not around, make sure that these objects are firmly secured. At bath time do not rush: most babies quickly get used to and enjoy the sensation of water being trickled over them, heads included. Encourage him to kick his legs and move his arms. When he is resting but awake, make sure he has room to move his arms, legs and head.

Memorise

Cover your face and play Peep-bo. This will help him get used to the idea that if you disappear from view you will come back.

As children learn by communicating with their world, we need to think about how they do this. They get information about their world by using all their senses and their memory.

Your child will need to have the opportunity to use all his senses to explore, to learn and to make sense of his world. At each stage of his infant life, think of the different situations he will encounter and consider how you can make sure he uses as many senses and skills as possible.

You want your baby to develop in an all round way, so:
- Have fun together
- Have confidence and experiment. You will be able to think up many more things to do with your baby than you will find in this book

Freedom to explore and learn in safety.

- Whatever the game or activity make sure you add the language to go with it. Keep listening for each new attempt your baby makes to communicate with you
- Obviously you need to be aware of any potential dangers in encouraging your child to explore and play. If you're not sure, use your common sense!

Your baby on the move

All too quickly babies learn to manipulate themselves, things around them and, very often, us as well! Our concern about possible dangers urges us to keep things out of reach and locked away. However, now is the time to provide more and more opportunity to experiment in safety.

The experiences listed on pages 25–28 still apply. In the following pages you will find activities and games to help your child develop further.

More activities and games for you and your baby

Time for you and time for me

WHAT TO DO

Work out a routine for each day and include different activities for you and your baby to enjoy. In this way you can gradually encourage your child to interact more and more with his world. He will begin to anticipate that things will happen at certain times eg clapping songs at nappy changing time, water play at bathtime etc.

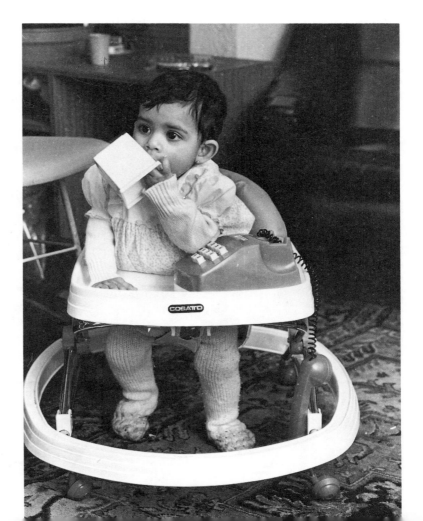

Babies absorb and learn a great deal by observing.

Baby Loot

YOU WILL NEED:
- a collection of things for handling eg a rattle, a mirror, soft toys, plastic rings, soft material block or brick, ball with bell in it. (When making your collection try to include a variety of colours, materials, sizes, shapes and things that make different sounds.)
- a bag or box to keep some of them in.

WHAT TO DO

Your baby will enjoy grasping them and as he gets older will learn to let things go and to drop them. He will also learn to bang one thing against another, to take turns to hand things to you after receiving them.

Good for:
- hand/eye coordination
- introducing the idea that things do exist even if out of sight. As you take things out of the box or bag he will begin to anticipate this. This is the beginning of thinking ahead.

Playing with small toys and objects helps babies to develop control of their hand movements.

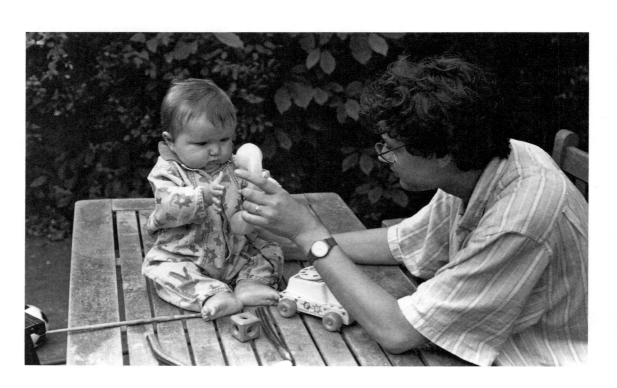

Unwrapping something needs even finer movement skills.

Surprise, surprise!

YOU WILL NEED:

- two or three small toys wrapped loosely in a few layers of colourful wrapping paper.

WHAT TO DO

Encourage your baby to unwrap the parcel.
   Good for:
- your baby to learn that things do exist even if he can't see them
- co-ordination, manipulating things with two hands.

You can make this type of activity more involved as your baby gets older and more active by adding a few more containers and parcels respectively. Objects used can vary in colour and size.
   Don't forget the language you can use, eg 'big', 'round', as well as comments to your baby.

A song for you and me

YOU WILL NEED:

- As well as songs you already know such as 'Pop goes the weasel', books like *Round And Round The Garden* by Sarah Williams (Oxford University Press, 1983) will give you ideas. See pages 50–51 for more useful books that contain examples.

WHAT TO DO

To start, choose a clapping song or rhyme that fits in with your baby's daily routine. An example is 'Clap, clap, hands', found in *Round And Round The Garden*. At first, you will have to clap your baby's hands for him at the appropriate time but soon he will be able to join in more and more. Add more when you feel he is ready.

Good for:
- co-ordination
- repetition
- anticipation
- memory of a sequence of events.

Make it happen

YOU WILL NEED:

- small plastic containers with no sharp edges. Place in each container either a bell, seeds or any small objects that will make different sounds when the containers are shaken. (Make sure the lids are secure!)

WHAT TO DO

The containers can either be suspended for the baby to hit, or held so that he can grasp, shake or roll them.

The same can be achieved with commercial toys that produce a sound or an action, eg a Jack-in-the-box, transparent balls or teething ring containing bells, plastic bench with holes for hammering shapes through.

Good for:
- your baby to learn that his action causes something to happen.
- learning to anticipate the effect of his action.

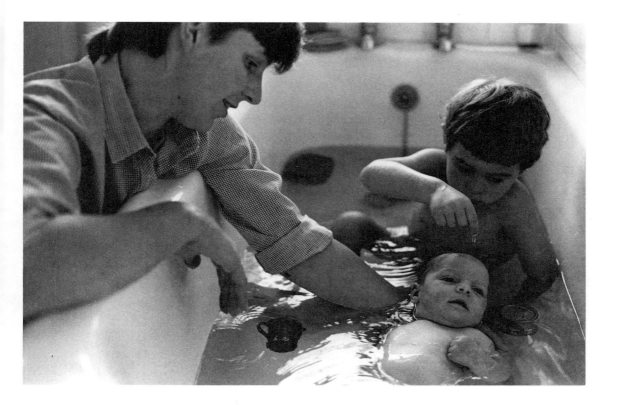

*There are lots of
opportunities for talking
and playing at bathtime!*

Fill it up and empty it out

This can be played at bathtime or at any time.
You will need:
- a large water container, eg bathtub, large bowl
- a variety of smaller containers of different sizes – yoghurt
  cartons, mugs, pots, stacking beakers
- water.

WHAT TO DO

Encourage your child to play with the water, filling and
emptying the containers.

When your baby is past the stage of putting things in the
mouth, you can substitute the water with such things as sand,
sugar or flour.

Good for:
- hand/eye co-ordination
- feeling the consistency of different substances
- the endless language possibilities.

Box it

YOU WILL NEED:

● two strong cardboard boxes (eg the types used to pack wine and spirits). They should be big enough for your baby to crawl through and into.

WHAT TO DO

Box 1: Remove the top flaps. Cover the raw edges with electrical tape of a contrasting colour. This box can double up as a toybox. It can be made cheerful by painting your baby's name on it and adding stick-on pictures. If you have the time, a coat of bright, non-toxic gloss paint lengthens the lives of the boxes and makes them brighter to look at. Make two holes at either end and thread pieces of thick cord through to make handles. Tie a knot at each end of each piece of cord.

Box 2: Remove the top and bottom flaps. Then, if you wish, decorate in the same way as Box 1.

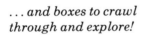

Boxes to pull and toys to sort . . .

. . . and boxes to crawl through and explore!

Throwing a ball is quite a difficult manipulative skill to learn.

WHAT TO DO

1 Encourage your baby to crawl in and out of the boxes.
2 Look out for when you see your baby pushing and pulling larger objects. Encourage him to push and pull the box.
3 Keep a few favourite toys in Box 1 and your baby will learn where his toys are kept, how to get them out, select his favourite and put them away.
4 Talk to him about what he is doing.

Good for:
● co-ordination
● organisation
● source for language development.

As he gets older you may prefer to replace the cardboard storage box with plastic containers. These tend to be less pliable and have harder edges that could hurt at the very early, unsteady stages of crawling and manœuvring.

As your child gets older more containers can be added and used to store different toys. This way he will learn to sort and keep things in order.

Catch 'n throw

YOU WILL NEED:
● a sponge ball.

WHAT TO DO

Encourage your baby to kick and throw the ball to you and to try to catch it when you throw it back.

Good for:
● concentration
● co-ordination
● introducing the language of action.

Things to look at and talk about

Pictures

Attractive pictures can be found in magazines, greetings cards, posters and gift wrapping paper. The latter provides some large colourful varieties for the wall, as well as smaller pictures to cut out. See pages 41–42 for more information.

Books

Introduce your baby to books as soon as he enjoys seeing the pictures. Take care when choosing books for him to handle. They will need to be tough, suckable, chewable and safe!

Show him the pictures and talk about the stories. Whenever possible show him the real equivalent of the pictures.

A mobile

There are many beautiful mobiles available to buy but one can easily be made quite cheaply and still look effective.

YOU WILL NEED:

● a frame. There are a number of ways to make one:
1 Join two pieces of dowelling (available at DIY stores) with cord or string.
2 Use a coat hanger or, if you're adventurous, two coat hangers attached to each other securely.
3 Use a hoop.

Hang a variety of objects from your frame, attaching them with threads of different lengths. Objects can range from pictures cut out of cards, to small toys or ornaments, shells and bells. Aim to include objects that vary in colour, size and shape. One idea is to choose objects that follow a theme, eg one or two colours, things that make a noise, metalllic objects etc.

Fix your mobile very securely and high up, out of your baby's reach. As he develops and is able to make things with your help, his work can be hung on the mobile. Change the things suspended from it from time to time.

Activities for working things out and making things

Does it fit?

YOU WILL NEED:

● a simple jigsaw which involves matching shapes with spaces. These can be made quite quickly using wrapping paper. See page 39.

There are various ways of making mobiles; older children can make them for baby brothers or sisters.

Good for:
- shape matching
- learning to do things by himself as well as with your help
- manipulative skills.

From the simple one-piece lift-out jigsaws, progress to ones with more pieces. From these move on to interlocking jigsaws with a few large pieces, and gradually go on to those with more and more pieces.

Build it up

YOU WILL NEED:

- stacking beakers, rings or blocks (available in toyshops). As an alternative, cereal boxes and other such items can be used.

WHAT TO DO

Encourage your child to build with them and talk about what he is doing.

Encourage your child to describe what he is doing when he is playing with you.

Good for:
- manipulative skills
- designing and building
- language development.

When your baby is able to fit things together it is worth considering buying (or borrowing) a construction set such as Duplo. This provides good preparation for more detailed construction kits for older children, eg Lego.

Sort it

YOU WILL NEED:

- a variety of objects or toys.

WHAT TO DO

1 Sort them by size. The language used might be 'big/small' and later 'bigger/smaller'.
2 Sort them by shape. Language might include 'round', 'square' etc.
3 Sort them by colour.
4 Sort them by texture. Language used might include 'soft', 'prickly', 'hard' etc.

Toys of different colours, shapes and textures provide lots of scope for developing language skills.

Make your own 'lift-out' jigsaw

YOU WILL NEED:

- a sheet of wrapping paper that has fairly large, clearly outlined shapes – for example, a paper with cats or cars or balloons of different sizes and colours. One sheet includes a repeat of the pattern. This could be used to make a number of jigsaws. See pages 41–42 for more information about wrapping papers.
- a large sheet of mounting card (available at stationery stores). This will probably be enough to make a number of jigsaws.

TO MAKE

1 Cut two pieces of the card the same size.
2 Glue the wrapping paper in a line along one of the card pieces (a spray adhesive is best as the paper will not wrinkle).
3 When dry, cut out each of the pictures/objects of the wrapping paper design, making sure that the outline of each shape is as accurate as possible. (A Stanley knife is easier to use than scissors.)
4 You will be left with a board with holes. Glue this to the other piece of mounting card.

WHAT TO DO

Match the piece with the space.
    Good for:

- hand/eye co-ordination
- matching shapes.

All by myself

Your baby will need a little time each day to play by himself. This is a good time for you to listen to what he says or see what he does – without being noticed, of course.

The little artist

Whether jigsaws are bought or made, they should be very simple shapes for young children.

YOU WILL NEED:

- a roll of lining paper (available from wallpaper and most DIY shops. I have found that lining paper is the cheapest way of getting large amounts of paper cheaply)

- finger paints (crayons, pencils etc can also be used)
- something to protect clothing.

WHAT TO DO

1 Make hand and foot prints. You will have to help your toddler do this at first.
2 Encourage him to transfer paint from the pots using his fingers. He will begin by enjoying feeling the consistency.

It may be messy but it's a good way of learning the fine motor skills necessary for writing!

3 Encourage him to make wavy and straight lines, patterns and shapes. Let him use whichever hand he wants to. Brushes can be used as well as fingers and hands.
A good book full of ideas is *Children's Art And Crafts* by Nancy Lewis. (Australian Consolidated Press)
Good for:
● fine motor control, necessary for developing writing skills later
● introducing more language linked with actions, colours etc.
   As co-ordination increases the activities above will be enjoyed for longer periods of time. As he grows, your toddler's concentration span will become longer, he will become more mobile and able to manipulate himself and the things around him.

Make believe

YOU WILL NEED:
● old clothes for dressing up.

WHAT TO DO
Encourage him to pretend to be someone else, to talk about who he is pretending to be and what he is pretending to do. Encourage him to use different voices for the different people.
   Good for:
● developing the imagination
● providing the opportunity for him to use language he has heard from others

Wrapping paper activities

When you look around the shops you will find there are all sorts of very attractive papers available in a variety of designs. These include large, complete pictures, familiar characters, the alphabet, animals, ships, Easter eggs and seasonal characters.
   Wrapping paper offers many possibilities. Below you will find two examples.

YOU WILL NEED:
two sheets of identical wrapping paper – the sort that has a complete picture on it and lots of detail.

A Stanley knife is the easiest way of cutting out home-made jigsaws.

WHAT TO DO

Mount both sheets on mounting a card using a spray adhesive (to prevent wrinkling). Keep one of the mounted sheets whole, for looking at and talking about.

The second can be used in a number of ways. For example, cut it up and use like a jigsaw. You can use the whole one to compare it with.

Find me in the picture

Cut one of the mounted cards into rectangles or characters and share the cards between you and your child. You take turns to turn up one of your cards. The other player looks at the other, whole one and asks questions in order to find which part of the picture you have.

Some wrapping papers to look out for

Medici Society
Dickinson Robinson Group Project
Woodland Animals Ltd
Gordon Frazer Wrapper
Dawn Publications
Gallery Five
Farhana Design and Co
Rainbow Designs
Elgin Court Designs Ltd, licensed by BBC Enterprises Ltd
Royle Publications Ltd
Image Arts of England

INTRODUCING THE WORLD OF BOOKS

It is never too early to start. Even before they can sit up, babies will listen to the tone and rhythms of words as you recite jingles, nursery rhymes and songs. Once he can sit on your lap, is ready to listen and to look at books, you can start to share fully the world of books with your baby, even though he is not yet talking. Books can help develop language: as you talk to your baby about the pictures, naming familiar objects and discussing what is happening, you will be laying the foundations of language which he can draw on as he begins to speak.

Books will also become familiar friends in their own right if they are part of life from the start, and you will be giving your child a firm footing when he starts school.

So how and what to choose from the thousands of children's books available today? The following booklists, and those at the end of each Part of this book, are an attempt to guide you through the labyrinth as you gaze at the well-stocked shelves in your local bookshop or library, rummage through old copies at jumble sales or flick through the pages of the book club catalogues. They are inevitably a personal selection but are representative of the best children's authors and illustrators. It is hoped that many of the titles in these lists will become family favourites, as they are for many children already.

Each list contains books suitable for the age range covered in the relevant chapter. As we all know, children develop at different rates and have widely different interests and needs, so we hope to have provided for these differences by including a variety of books of varying interest and level of difficulty. The division into age range categories should be taken *as a rough guide and not stuck to rigidly*. Some books may be suitable for older or younger children as well as the age group we have suggested it for. A book you read to your child when he was three may be one he learns to read later on!

When selecting any of these titles, always bear *your* child in mind: *his* likes and *his* stage of development. It is also very important to give your *child* a say in which books are chosen. Personal taste is developed by allowing children to choose from the start. Even if you do not agree with your child's choice of library book, don't say 'No'; let him take the book and discover whether he likes it or not. Choose what you consider to be a more suitable book as well, and you will both be satisfied.

Note: All books listed are sold in paperback unless otherwise stated. Dates refer to the edition mentioned, not to the original date of publication.

Board books

Board books are the ideal introduction to the world of books for babies: attractive, fun to handle, hard-wearing and easy to wipe clean. With them you can introduce babies to what books are for and how to handle them. And you can also show them the pleasure they can bring.

The Animal Directory *Rodney Peppé*
   Blackie 1989
Bold, simple, coloured pictures of animals with a large thumb index of numbers 1 to 10 – just right for a baby's podgy thumbs! A lovely first counting book.

Big Board Books:
All Fall Down; Clap Hands; Say Goodnight; Tickle Tickle. *Helen Oxenbury*
   Walker 1987
Larger-than-usual board books with large, clear, coloured drawings of a multi-cultural collection of babies doing all sorts of things for your baby to imitate.

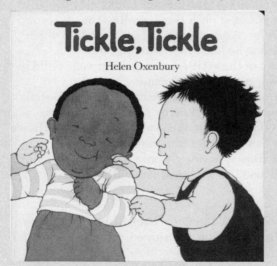

Bruna Chunky Books *Dick Bruna*
   Methuen 1989
Chunky little books with Dick Bruna's simple shapes and bold coloured pictures. No words but lots for you to talk about.

First Board Books:
Toys; Pets; Zoo Animals; Farm Animals.
   Blackie 1988
Bright, glossy colour photographs of familiar objects and animals.

Nursery Board Books:
Homes; 123; ABC; Weather; Farm. *Jan Pienkowski*
   Heinemann 1988
Tiny books in bright primary colours. Excellent for naming and vocabulary development.

Opposites:
Wet-Dry; Fat-Thin; In-Out; On-Off. *Illustrated by Colin McNaughton*
   Sainsbury's 1986
A fun way to learn about opposites with amusing pictures.

Novelty books

Children will be entranced by books that you can squeeze, books with holes and books with flaps to lift.

Animal Shapes *Joanna Troughton*
   Blackie 1986
Cardboard concertina books, beautifully illustrated by Joanna Troughton.

My Big Bath Books:
My Rocket; My Submarine.
   Collins 1988
Large plastic 'books' in the shape of a rocket and a submarine. More for playing with in the bath than for reading, but they do encourage babies to turn the 'pages'.

Cuddly Books:
Off We Go; My Clothes; On The Farm; In The Garden.
   Collins 1987
These first naming 'books' are made of sponge pages covered in cloth, with a brightly coloured picture and word on each 'page'. More for going to sleep with than a real book – and eminently suckable! (The colours are 'non-toxic'.) Perhaps being able to suck, chew and dribble on this sort of book will encourage children to grow up thinking of books as friends!

Dear Zoo *Rod Campbell*
    Picture Puffin 1984
Children will have fun guessing which pet the zoo has
sent and lifting the flap on each page to see if they were
right.

I Can Blink; I Can Roar *Frank Asch*
    Picture Corgi 1989
These books have a hole big enough for a child's face,
through which they can make the appropriate animal
noises and grimaces as the pages are turned.

My Book; Is Anyone Home? *Ron Maris*
    Picture Puffin 1985
These delightful books with half-page flaps entice
children into guessing what comes next.

Soft Cuddly Big Softies:
Dog; Cat; Bear; Rabbit.
    Blackie
Large, spongy, cloth-covered books, each about a
different animal. These animals have real
personalities, which is more than can be said for most
pictures in cloth books.

**Spot's Birthday; Spot's First Walk; Where's
Spot?** *Eric Hill*
    Picture Puffin 1983
The best of the bestselling stories about the doings of
this endearing little puppy. Youngsters love lifting
flaps to see what's behind, no matter how many times
they have done it before.

The Very Hungry Caterpillar *Eric Carle*
    Picture Puffin 1974
A modern classic. Children delight in seeing how the
caterpillar munches his way through heaps of food in
order to change into a butterfly – via flaps, and a small
hole where the caterpillar has been!

Picture books without words

This kind of book is an excellent way of
showing a young child two important things
they need to learn about books:
1 how to look closely and tell a story from
   the pictures,
2 how we look at pictures in a book from
   left to right and from top to bottom.
Talking about the pictures together and
taking turns in telling the story will help to
develop your child's language, interest in
stories and a confident attitude towards
books.

The Gift *John Prater*
 Picture Puffin 1987
Two children receive a present in a huge cardboard box. They have a wonderful time in the box, which can fly. It takes them on an exciting journey round the world.

Little Pickle *Peter Collington*
 Magnet 1988
A day in the life of the mischievous Little Pickle who dreams she goes to sea and meets the fishermen on board a fishing boat. Each page has a different arrangement of pictures which will provide lots to talk about and practice in 'reading' pictures in sequence.

The Snowman *Raymond Briggs*
 Picture Puffin 1980
The book from which the now-famous film was made. If you do not know the book, get it. It's a magical experience sharing this book with a child.

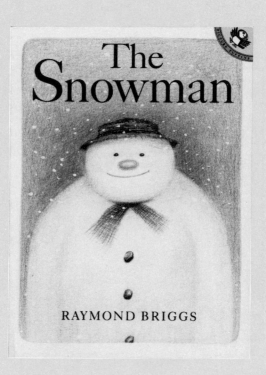

Sunshine; Moonlight *Jan Ormerod*
 Picture Puffin 1983
Two gently funny books about a little girl and her mum and dad. One is about getting up and one about going to bed.

The Trunk *Brian Wildsmith*
 OUP 1982
The bold pictures tell a simple story with a surprising ending about animals climbing up a trunk.
 See also **Whose Shoes?**, **The Nest** and **The Apple Bird**.

Books to share with your child: ages 0–4

All the books for children aged 0–4 (except, perhaps, the 'read-alouds' and some of the rhyme books) are to share; that is, for you and your child to sit together side by side or with your child on your lap while you read the story and your child looks at the pictures, joins in and talks about it. This section contains picture books for sharing.

Alfie Gets In First *Shirley Hughes*
 Picture Lion 1982
Alfie gets locked in the house. We see Mum and Annie Rose outside on the front doorstep and Alfie on the other side of the door. Also **Alfie's Feet**.

The Baby's Catalogue *Janet & Allan Ahlberg*
 Picture Puffin 1984
A must as a 'talking with baby' book. Hours of fun sharing familiar experiences in five different babies' lives.

Bear Hunt; Bear Goes To Town *Anthony Browne*
 Hippo 1982 Sparrow 1983
Bear uses his magic pencil to draw himself out of tricky situations. Anthony Browne is an author/illustrator whose pictures demand close inspection and reveal more on each occasion. His bizarre images in everyday settings challenge adult preconceptions and delight children's open minds.

Bear Shadow *Frank Asch*
   Picture Corgi 1989
Bear's shadow gets in his way when he is fishing. He tries every way he can to get rid of it. Watch out for the many other books about this delightful little bear.

A Bun For Barney *Joyce Dunbar*
   Picture Corgi 1989
Barney's bun starts off with five cherries on it but he gradually loses them out of generosity to other creatures.

John Burningham's Colours Book
   Walker 1988
Big print and pictures introduce the young child to a new colour on each page.

Coming To Tea; Doing The Washing; Going Shopping; Having A Picnic *Sarah Garland*
   Picture Puffin 1985
Sarah Garland's energetic drawings bring to life a busy, sometimes harassed mum and her two children in familiar, everyday situations.

Daisy Tales: Daisy And The Crying Baby; Daisy And The Babysitter; Daisy And The Washing Machine; Daisy Goes Swimming *Tony Bradman & Priscilla Lamont*
   Picture Knight 1989
Four little picture books about a charming toddler in familiar situations.

Ernest And Celestine *Gabrielle Vincent*
   Picture Lion 1983
Ernest the bear looks after his friend, Celestine, a litte mouse.

Good Morning, Chick *Mirra Ginsburg*
   Picture Corgi 1986
The first day in the life of a little chick who explores the farm, with his mother looking on. On the left-hand page is the story for you to read and opposite is a boldly coloured picture with the repeated words 'like this' for children to join in with.

Hairy Maclary From Donaldson's Dairy *Lynley Dodd*
   Picture Puffin 1985
Little Hairy Maclary goes for a walk and meets other doggy friends who join him until they meet Scarface Claw, the toughest Tom in town. Impossible to resist joining in with this brilliant rhyming story. Also: **Hairy Maclary's Bone; Hairy Maclary Scattercat** and **Hairy Maclary's Caterwaul Caper**.

How Do I Put It On? *Shigeo Watanabe*
   Picture Puffin 1981
The antics of this endearing little bear will delight all toddlers – both those learning to dress themselves and those who have already mastered the art! There are many other titles about the same bear.

It's Mine *Leo Lionni*
   Picture Knight 1989
Old toad helps the young frogs learn to share.

Ladybird, Ladybird *Ruth Brown*
   Beaver 1989
A sumptuously illustrated long version of the well-known children's rhyme.

Maisie Middleton *Nita Sowter*
    Picture Lion 1982
Toddlers love Maisie's mischievous antics as she makes
her own wonderful breakfast after rejecting Dad's burnt
offering.

My Day *Rod Campbell*
    Picture Lion 1986
Follow the baby in the book through his day and name
all the things he meets, from getting up to going to bed.

On Friday Something Funny Happened *John Prater*
    Picture Puffin 1984
This sounds like an ordinary week in the life of a small
brother and sister but the pictures reveal a rather
different story – great naughtiness until they get to
Friday!

Peace At Last *Jill Murphy*
    Picturemac 1982
Mr Bear can't get to sleep wherever he tries because
there is too much noise. Children will love joining in
the repeated phrase: 'Oh NO!' said Mr Bear, 'I can't
stand THIS.'

The Perfect Day *John Prater*
    Picture Corgi 1989
The whole family have a wonderful day at the seaside –
everyone, that is, except Kevin!

Pets/Farm Animals *Colin Hawkins*
    Macmillan 1989
Two simple naming books in one – just flip the book
over and start again from the back.

A Porcupine Named Fluffy *Helen Lester*
    Picturemac 1989
Mr and Mrs Porcupine call their son Fluffy but he soon
finds he isn't. He tries all sorts of ways of becoming
fluffy until he meets a rhinoceros with an equally
inappropriate name. The superlatively witty drawings
of Fluffy by Lyn Munsinger make this book a real treat.

Rosie's Walk *Pat Hutchins*
    Picture Puffin 1970
The magic of this modern classic lies in the pictures
which show the reader so much more than the simple
words of the story tell. The child can see what Rosie
the hen cannot see happening behind her back.
Without realising it, Rosie defeats the fox at every turn.

Titch; You'll Soon Grow Into Them, Titch *Pat
Hutchins*
    Picture Puffin 1985
Two stories about the youngest child in a family. Told
in simple language with pictures that tell so much more.

Tom And Pippo Books *Helen Oxenbury*
    Walker 1988
A series of books about Tom and his toy monkey in
familiar, everyday situations.

Two Shoes, New Shoes *Shirley Hughes*
    Walker 1988
A delightful rhyming text and cosy pictures show
children dressing up in all sorts of clothes. This is one
of a series by Shirley Hughes called *The Nursery
Collection*. All are equally good.

Welcome, Little Baby *Aliki*
    Picture Piper 1989
A lovely first book for new parents to read to their baby,
or for an older child who has just had a new baby
brother or sister.

We're Going On A Bear Hunt *Michael Rosen & Helen
Oxenbury*
    Walker 1989 Hardback
This brilliant adaptation of an action rhyme will have
children joining in with the first reading and demanding
it again and again. Dad, children, baby and dog wade
through long grass, squelch through mud etc on their
bear hunt and end up just a little bit scared but safe
back in bed.

What's The Time, Mr Wolf? *Colin Hawkins*
    Picture Lion 1986
Mr Wolf, with his manic appetite, introduces the child
to telling the time as he goes through his day. The very
large, bold print and repeated phrases also make this a
good book for beginner readers and partially-sighted
children.
    Also: **Mr Wolf's Week** in which disaster strikes Mr
Wolf every day. A fun way to learn the days of the
week.

When I'm Sleepy *Jane R. Howard*
    Beaver 1987
A lovely bedtime book with sumptuous pictures by
Lynne Cherry.

Each Peach Pear Plum *Janet & Allan Ahlberg*
Picture Lion 1980
A great favourite. Clever and amusing illustrations in which children have to look very carefully to find nursery rhyme and fairy tale characters.

Peepo! *Janet and Allan Ahlberg*
Picture Puffin 1983
A hole in the page reveals a tiny part of what the baby sees in his 1940s home. Turn the page to see the whole picture.

Where Do The Wicked Witches Live? *Juliet & Charles Snape*
Picture Corgi 1988
Dennis goes far and wide to find the wicked witches but he doesn't see them anywhere. We can find them and other creatures on each page if we look carefully.

Counting books

Anno's Counting Book *Mitsumasa Anno*
Picturemac 1985
The beautiful, cool paintings by Mitsumasa Anno are a delight. They show a country scene which changes as you turn the pages. Not only are there more things to count to each page but the scene also goes through the seasons.

Joe Can Count *Jan Ormerod*
Walker 1990
A delightful first counting book, showing a little black boy counting animals up to ten using language which comes tripping off the tongue, eg 'ten playful piglets'.

1 Hunter *Pat Hutchins*
Picture Puffin 1984
An I-Spy book, a counting book and an adventure story all rolled into one as we (and the animals) follow the hunter through the jungle.

The Midnight Farm *Reeve Lindbergh*
Picture Puffin 1989
A beautiful, warm book, illustrated by Susan Jeffers, which children will want to return to again and again. A mother takes her son round the farm to count the animals in the night. Reassuring for a child afraid of the dark.

One Bear All Alone *Caroline Bucknall*
Picturemac 1987
From 'One bear all alone, sitting by the telephone', we count up to ten bears in rhyming couplets.

One Bear At Bedtime *Mick Inkpen*
Picture Knight 1989
A delightful bedtime animal counting book.

Ten In A Bed *Mary Rees*
Little Mammoth 1989
A comic version of the well-known song with the little one who said 'Roll over, roll over'. Also good for learning to read later. It counts back from ten to nought.

Ten, Nine, Eight *Molly Bang*
Picture Puffin 1985
A cosy and loving countdown to bedtime with a black father and his daughter.

ABC books

ABC Word Book *Richard Scarry*
  Collins 1972 Hardback
Lots of little animals are busy on every page in the
usual Scarry way. There is lots to look at, talk about
and read.

The Baby Animal ABC *Robert Broomfield*
  Picture Puffin 1968
An ideal first alphabet for the very young and an
opportunity to learn the names of animals and their
young as well.

John Burningham's Alphabet Book
  Walker 1988
This is a first ABC book which has one simple drawing
for each letter of the alphabet, mostly of animals.

Lucy and Tom's ABC *Shirley Hughes*
  Picture Puffin 1985
We really feel we know Shirley Hughes' characters,
they are so human and alive – and Lucy and her little
brother, Tom, are no exception. This alphabet shows us
and tells us about their family, friends and
neighbourhood with warm, humorous drawings and
text.

Mog's Amazing Birthday Caper *Judith Kerr*
  Picture Lion 1985
Judith Kerr's lovable cat, Mog, goes through the
alphabet from 'Mog accidentally ate an alligator . . .' to
'Out of the zigzag zip-bag zooms something to guzzle
. . .' An ABC which tells a proper story.

**The Most Amazing Hide And Seek Alphabet
Book** *Robert Crowther*
  Viking 1987 Hardback
This certainly is a most amazing book! Children never
tire of pushing, pulling and lifting the flaps to reveal
the animals hidden behind each letter. Worth every
penny.

Brian Wildsmith's ABC
  OUP
A sumptuous first alphabet, painted in rich colours on
dark glossy paper. One picture on a page with the name
printed opposite in both capitals and lower case letters.

Nursery rhymes and action rhymes

**Nicola Bayley's Nonsense Rhymes; Nicola Bayley's
Bedtime Rhymes**
  Walker 1989
Two exquisitely illustrated little books which have one
rhyme on each left-hand page and a beautiful painting
to go with it on the right.

**Boys And Girls Come Out To Play; Oranges And
Lemons; Polly Put The Kettle On; Ring A Ring A
Roses**
  Carnival 1988
Each of these inexpensive little books has about 15
nursery songs and rhymes, one per page with a
(somewhat dated) colour illustration opposite. They are
just the right size for a young child to handle and the
clear print and uncluttered layout make them ideal for
early reading books later after the child has learnt
them by heart.

Clap Your Hands; Stamp Your Feet *Chosen by Sarah
Hayes*
  Walker 1989
Two delightful collections of action rhymes and finger
rhymes. Toni Goffe's humorous pictures cleverly tell
the story of the rhyme *and* show the actions.

The Faber Book Of Nursery Verse *Edited by Barbara
Ireson*
  Faber 1983
A really comprehensive volume full of rhymes and
simple poems for reading aloud. Few illustrations.

Hand Rhymes *Collected and drawn by Marc Brown*
  Picture Lion 1987
One illustrated rhyme on each double spread. There is
a little diagram by each line to show you what actions
to do.

Lavender's Blue *Compiled by Kathleen Lines*
  OUP 1989
Packed with hundreds of traditional favourite nursery
rhymes and pictures. There is an index and instructions
for accompanying actions to some rhymes.

Mother Goose *Brian Wildsmith*
    OUP 1987
All the favourites, colourfully illustrated by Brian Wildsmith in his unmistakable style.

Oranges And Lemons *Compiled by Karen King*
    OUP 1986
Group songs and dancing games. Instructions and music are clearly set out on the left-hand page; the verses, illustrated by Ian Beck, are on the right.

Out And About *Shirley Hughes*
    Walker 1990
A very first poetry book for the young, lovingly illustrated by Shirley Hughes. A visual and verbal treat to treasure.

Over The Moon *Chosen by Charlotte Voake*
    Walker 1989
A well-laid out book of rhymes with clear print and lovely, lively drawings by Charlotte Voake

Rhymes Around The Day *Chosen by Pat Thomson*
    Picture Puffin 1985
A lovely little collection of first rhymes, some traditional some modern, illustrated by Jan Ormerod.

Ride A Cock Horse *Chosen by Sarah Williams*
    OUP 1988
This collection is subtitled 'knee-jogging rhymes, patting songs and lullabies'. They are exactly that – very rhythmical and rocking rhymes! Illustrated. Also: **Round And Round The Garden**.

This Little Puffin *Compiled by Elizabeth Matterson*
    Puffin 1969
Deservedly still in print. The is *the* collection of finger play, singing games and action rhymes. If you can get only one action rhyme book – buy this one.

**A First Treasury Of Nursery Rhymes;
A Second Treasury Of Nursery Rhymes** *Edited by Michael Foss*
    Picturemac 1988
These books are subtitled 'with classic illustrations'. Some children may find the pictures rather old-fashioned while mum and dad may enjoy them more.

Books to read aloud

Andrew McAndrew
Bernard MacLaverty
    Walker Read Aloud 1989
Eight delightful short stories about Andrew who loves making up rhymes. Things tend to go wrong whenever he visits his grandad.

Bread And Jam For Frances *Russell Hoban*
    Picture Puffin 1977
Frances is fussy and will only eat bread and jam, so Mother gives it to her every day at every meal until Frances cannot stand the sight of it any longer and asks for spaghetti and meatballs like the rest of the family. Parents and young children will relate to this and other growing-up problems in the *Frances* books.

Dogger *Shirley Hughes*
    Picture Lion 1979
Dave is heartbroken when he loses his much-loved cuddly toy, Dogger.

The Helen Oxenbury Nursery Story Book
   Young Lion 1989
Ten well-loved traditional tales such as *The Gingerbread Boy* and *The Three Billy Goats Gruff* told in a chatty style which cries out to be read aloud with all the different voices. A grown-up with dramatic leanings will have a ball!

Owl And Billy *Martin Waddell*
   Magnet 1988
Billy is waiting to start school. He and Owl (his soft toy, made from a stuffed pillowcase) make friends with a motorbike-riding spaceman who moves into the old folk's bungalows down the road.

Postman Pat's Winter Storybook *John Cunliffe*
   Hippo 1989
A bumper book: six stories in one about this much-loved television character. There are many more books about him, all published by Scholastic Hippo.

The Read-Aloud Treasury *Compiled by Joanna Cole & Stephanie Calmenson*
   Michael O'Mara 1989 Hardback
A boldly illustrated collection of poems, nursery rhymes, traditional tales and modern stories which children will want to hear over and over again.

Stories For Under-Fives *Edited by Sara & Stephen Corrin*
   Puffin 1979
The Corrins have put together this collection of short stories which are just right for that odd quiet moment and always end on a safe and happy note.

The Three Bears And 15 Other Stories *Selected and illustrated by Anne Rockwell*
   Puffin 1989
A chunky little book containing a collection of 16 well-known nursery tales, brightly illustrated by the author.

The Walker Fairy Tale Library Books 1–12 *Retold by Sarah Hayes*
   Walker 1988
Each volume contains three or four well-told stories, ranging from nursery tales to folk tales and Greek myths. A library worth building, they are beautifully produced and full of pictures by many different artists. Books to grow with your child.

Where The Wild Things Are *Maurice Sendak*
   Picture Puffin 1970
Not for the *very* young, but children do like to be just a little bit frightened as long as everything goes back to normal at the end. The story does just that in this modern classic about naughty Max who has a wild rumpus with some very fierce looking monsters but ends up back in his bedroom with his supper waiting for him, still hot.

Wilberforce Goes To Playgroup *Margaret Gordon*
   Picture Puffin 1989
Hilarious pictures show Wilberforce's first action-packed day at playgroup. They are made even funnier by the very matter-of-fact way the story is told. For other 'everyday' happenings in this little bear's life see also: *Wilberforce Goes On A Picnic*; *Wilberforce Goes Shopping* and *Wilberforce Goes To A Party*.

Books for playing I-Spy or 'Can you see . . .?'

Where Is Bobo?
Susan Hulme & Jan Siegieda
   Magnet 1987
Colour photographs tell the story of a day in Sam's life. Spot his teddy on each page.

But Where Is The Green Parrot? *Thomas & Wanda Zacharias*
   Piccolo 1972
A good book for learning colour words, joining in with the repeated phrase 'BUT WHERE IS THE GREEN PARROT?' and finding the green parrot in each picture.

This four-year-old has already learned that books are a source of pleasure and is ready to make a start on reading.

2 STARTING TO READ:
ages 5–7

Infant classrooms are lively places with lots of books waiting to be discovered.

The point at which any one child recognises, understands and remembers a word or groups of words could be said to be the first evidence that reading has begun. For some children this will be at three, for others four and for others five or even later. The important thing to remember is that words are best learned in a meaningful context – the child's own name because it is written under a photograph or on a greetings card, or the well-loved stories that you have been reading and sharing with

your child. Sharing and re-reading books with your child is the most profitable, pleasurable and painless way of learning to read. Words that are remembered and gradually recognised in one context are slowly remembered and recognised in others until they are 'established' and can be recognised in any context or, finally, in isolation. By now your child will probably be joining in with you as you read and will be able to:

- recognise favourite books
- turn the pages for you
- join in with you on rhymes or repeated phrases in a story
- 'read' a story from the pictures, but not match the language he uses with the actual text
- recognise some of the words because the book is known well and words are guessed correctly and remembered
- look at the books you have shared later on when he is alone – perhaps 'reading' the story aloud, ie memorising or summarising it or actually remembering and pointing to certain parts or phrases.

This knowledge is built upon as children learn to read in school and continue their reading development with you at home.

READING IN SCHOOL

1989 saw the introduction of the National Curriculum for all five-year-olds in state schools in England and Wales. Within just a few years it will apply to pupils of all ages up to 16. It is a time of great change and preparation for schools.

The National Curriculum maps out the knowledge and understanding that children are expected to acquire as they progress through various levels of achievement in most school subjects. It consists of three core subjects: English, mathematics and science and seven other foundation subjects such as history, music, art, technology and geography. All children must follow these subjects up to the age of 16.

Let's take a more detailed look at English in the National Curriculum which, even though it applies only to England and Wales, is similar to the requirements for Scotland and Northern Ireland. The following extracts are from *English in the National Curriculum* and reproduced with the permission of the Controller of Her Majesty's Stationery Office.

English is split into what are described as three profile components: Speaking and listening, Reading and Writing.

There are five Attainment Targets (ATs) at Key Stage 1 which is for five to seven-year-olds. These are:

AT 1 – Speaking and listening:

'The development of pupils' understanding of the spoken word and the capacity to express themselves effectively in a variety of speaking and listening activities, matching style and response to audience and purpose.'

AT 2 – Reading:

'The development of the ability to read, understand and respond to all types of writing, as well as the development of information-retrieval strategies for the purposes of study.'

AT 3 – Writing:

'A growing ability to construct and convey meaning in written language matching style to audience and purpose.'

AT 4 – Spelling

AT 5 – Handwriting

Each Attainment Target is split into ten levels – Level Two being the standard expected of the average seven-year-old. Within each level there are detailed statements of attainment which describe what children should be able to do in order to achieve that level of that Attainment Target.

For example: Level Two – Reading:

- 'read accurately and understand straightforward signs, labels and notices
- demonstrate knowledge of the alphabet in using word books and simple dictionaries
- use picture and context cues, words recognised on sight and phonic cues in reading.
  (Example: 'Use a picture to help make sense of a text; recognise that "Once" is often followed by "upon a time"; use initial letters to help with recognising words.')
- describe what has happened in a story and predict what may happen next
- listen and respond to stories, poems and other material read aloud, expressing opinions informed by what has been read
- read a range of material with some independence, fluency, accuracy and understanding.'

Programmes of Study are also set out which schools must follow. They give information and examples of the sorts of things teachers should be doing and providing for their pupils. The Programmes of Study tell teachers what they should be teaching but not how. That is left to their professional judgement – as long as children are following the broad paths the National Curriculum lays down.

Reading is a good example of this. There are three main organisational approaches to the teaching of reading in use in schools. All are acceptable under the National Curriculum *as long as* children have the access to different books and the variety of reading experiences that the National Curriculum for English requires. The three broad approaches are:

Reading schemes

This usually means that one scheme forms a framework or broad path for children to follow. Described as the use of a core scheme, it means that a reading scheme forms the core or spine of the language and reading work – but not *all* of it. Schemes that can be used like this include *Reading 360, One Two Three and Away! Reading World* and *Oxford Reading Tree*. Such schemes have various support materials, eg stories on tape, workbooks/worksheets, games and, naturally, support and suggestions for the teacher as well as books arranged in developmental levels.

It must be stressed that the books from the scheme are not the only books a child would be reading because no matter how good any scheme is it cannot possibly provide *all* the reading experiences and variety that a child should have.

Most schools have several reading schemes which may be used in different ways. For example: sometimes other schemes are used to consolidate progress on a main scheme, or children use particular schemes according to their likes and interests, or they are simply there as reading books.

Individualised Reading

This is when books are grouped into levels of difficulty by the staff and the reading material is then often colour-coded with labels to indicate which level they are at: eg all the books with a pink label are all roughly the same level of difficulty. Books from a variety of sources are used – from single title fiction such as *Picture Puffin* books to selected series and schemes.

Teachers share books with children just as parents do.

Children choose their books mainly from the level which is deemed to be appropriate for their stage of development. They may, however, choose easier or harder books if they wish – in the latter case they receive some support with their reading, from their parents, for example.

Ungraded collections of books

This is sometimes known as a 'Real Books' approach to reading, meaning that books from reading schemes are not used. Schools operating this approach have collections of books which are not graded in any way at all. Children select whatever book they want. If it is one that is too difficult for them to read alone (as it will be at the early stages, in particular) then they receive support from the teacher or someone else – sharing and re-reading the book.

This is known as an 'Apprenticeship Approach' to reading:

the skilled reader provides the model for the child to follow; the novice learns alongside the skilled tutor as the name suggests.

WHY DO SCHOOLS CHOOSE ONE APPROACH IN PREFERENCE TO ANOTHER?

Schools tend to use the approach that their members of staff feel happiest with – that they deem to be both successful and practical. The approach must also fit with what the staff believe about children learning to read.

At one time almost all children learned to read using a reading scheme and precious little else in the way of other books. Children may have learned the skills of reading but in the process they may also have learned that books were not very exciting things. They did not, therefore, become readers in the fullest sense of the word.

Approaches such as 'Individualised Reading' and 'Real Books' largely arose for three reasons:

1 The dissatisfaction with the then available reading schemes, many of which used unnatural and stilted language (eg 'See, see, see the balloon. Up, up, up.'). They also tended to have very little in the way of storylines, and characters were often, at best, pale, stereotyped shadows of the real world.
2 A recognition that if children are to become readers who turn to books readily and with pleasure, they need to become 'hooked' on books at an early age by being exposed to the joys, richness and variety they can provide.
3 It seemed a more natural way for children to learn to read.

Reading schemes, however, can and do provide a structure of development which can help the teacher – who, remember, has to teach an entire curriculum, not just reading. In recent years the newly published schemes have attempted to provide books which children thoroughly enjoy, a much greater variety of content, a framework to help teachers and they are grounded in a better understanding of what is involved in learning to read. Schemes that manage this include *Storychest*, *Oxford Reading Tree*, *Longman Reading World* and *Bookshelf* (in order of publication). All the authors and publishers of these schemes recognise the need for children to be reading other books as well.

Having good schemes available does help schools to make a

"YES . . . under the chair!"

"Are you in the bedroom, hairy bear, hairy bear, are 14 you in the bedroom . . . ?"

15

An example from a recently published reading scheme, Where's my hairy bear? *by Wendy Body in Longman Reading World, Longman 1990.*

genuine choice as to which approach they will adopt. At the moment the vast majority of schools use either reading schemes, 'Individualised Reading' or a mixture of both. Fewer schools use an ungraded approach – probably because it demands a lot of one-to-one support and, therefore, extra pairs of hands in the classroom.

IS ANY ONE OF THESE APPROACHES MORE EFFECTIVE THAN THE OTHERS?

There is no hard evidence to suggest that this is so. All approaches produce some failures as well as their many successes. That is not surprising. There will always be some children who experience difficulty in learning to read, *Whatever* approach is used. Such children need a change of approach in order to then succeed.

WHAT ABOUT PHONICS?

Teaching and learning phonics is about teaching and learning the sound-to-symbol system of the language – knowing that certain letters or groups of letters are likely to be pronounced in certain ways.

At one time, schools used to adopt either a look-say or a phonic approach to reading – learning words as whole units through repetition or learning words by breaking them down into their sounds: eg 'cr-ee-p'→'creep'. Our thinking has moved on somewhat and teachers now understand that this was an over-simplification. Children do need to acquire some understanding of the sound-symbol system of the language. So they do, in some way, need some phonics teaching in order to help in dealing with unfamiliar words.

The most important aspect of this is learning about initial sounds – individual letters and two/three letter combinations such as *st, cr, sh, spl*. The reason this is the most important aspect is as follows:

When children come to an unfamiliar word they are taught to predict or guess what the word might be. They must learn how to predict or guess effectively and not rely on wild or haphazard guesses. They are shown how to miss out the word, read on or re-read and then go back (thus using context and meaning to help them guess) and also to use the sounds at the beginning of the word as an extra clue.

In practice, this might work as follows:

It was cold out so she put on her warm ——.

The context or sense of the sentence helps us to guess that the missing word is an item of clothing – *scarf, jacket, coat, jumper, gloves* would all make sense and be grammatically correct. If we add some more information to the missing word:

It was cold out so she put on her warm ju——,

then we can be pretty certain what the word actually is (jumper); the information carried by the first letters of the word helps us make accurate predictions.

The Programme of Study for Reading in the National Curriculum is specific about the way children should be helped to deal with unfamiliar words and this is dealt with in the advice on pages 70–71. It is not recommended or even suggested that children should use phonic skills in order to sound out or build up words: 'c-r-a-b'→'crab'.

The reason for this is that a large number of words in English do not follow the common 'rules': eg done, put, was, women. Teaching a child to sound out words will not always work and so it is a technique that cannot be relied upon. The child who cannot read 'beautiful' or 'flashing' *does not know* that phonics will work for one but not for the other. The inevitable result? Confusion! Using knowledge about letter patterns and sounds (sh, ing, er etc) in order to make or check an educated guess is, however, a different matter.

In some shape or form then, all schools do some phonics teaching. This may, for example, be playing games such as Bingo with letter sounds, or looking for a common pattern in a list of known words or some direct teaching about, say, the sound of *ch* because it arises while a child is reading to the teacher.

Reading time in school

There are many teaching and learning experiences related to reading which go on in school every day. These may include:
- reading to the teacher from a personal reading book
- sharing a book and reading with the teacher in a small group
- pairs of children reading to and with each other
- playing reading games to reinforce specific teaching points
- making a book to share with others
- putting sentences or chunks of text into the correct sequence
- matching pictures/words/sentences
- listening to a story on tape and following it in the book
- listening and discussing a story read by the teacher
- looking at simple information books to find out about a topic.

Every one of these experiences teaches a child something about reading. A child is not only learning to read when he is reading to the teacher. Reading to the teacher is a time for the teacher to monitor a child's progress and see how the child's skills are developing in order to plan what to do next. It is not simply to provide practice for the child.

HOW OFTEN CAN YOU EXPECT YOUR CHILD
TO READ TO THE TEACHER?

Well it depends on the number of children in the class and what percentage of the day the teacher is able to devote to this activity. Let's assume that there are 30 children in the class and that the teacher devotes half an hour or roughly 10 per

Teachers listen to children reading to monitor how they are getting on and to plan for their next stage of development.

cent of his or her day to this task (remember all the other things that have to be taught!). Realistically, if the teacher is to get sufficient information to make a reading session worthwhile, he or she needs to spend five minutes with each child (bearing in mind that there are inevitable interruptions from other children!). This means that the teacher can listen to six children reading per day, which, in turn, means that an individual child can be seen once a week for this purpose. That may not seem very often to you, but do remember that any child will be doing lots of other things as well which are refining and extending his reading skills (like the activities listed above).

You and the school

Most schools expect children to take books home and they hope that parents will share the books with their children and listen to them read (see page 67). Not only does this provide additional practice for your child, but it also helps to strengthen home–school links.

Some schools ask parents to jot down in a special notebook or on a card their child's reactions to a book and any difficulties which may have been experienced. This helps the teacher by providing information, from another viewpoint, about a child's reading. Even if your child's school does not operate such a system, the class teacher always welcomes discussion with a parent about a child's reading.

Please don't ever be afraid to talk to your child's teacher about any worries or concerns you may have. For example, you may think that a particular book is too hard for your child or that he seems to have been bringing the same book home for far too long. Teachers are not all-powerful, all-knowing beings – they are *human* beings! When you have 30 or so children in your care the odd hiccup is bound to occur. It is so important to talk to the class teacher – that way tiny little problems can be sorted out quickly and easily before they escalate into something which is bigger and harder to resolve. Don't worry that the teacher will think you are fussing or making mountains out of molehills. Every teacher I know (and I know a lot) welcomes parents to come and talk things over and report on progress and problems.

It may not be hard for a parent to catch a teacher and say: 'Carolyn loved the book she brought home last night – are there any more like this one?' but it may be very hard to talk to the teacher if you feel there is something wrong. Perhaps these hints may help:

1 If possible, *arrange* to talk to the teacher rather than grab him at the start of a busy day or when he is supposed to be rushing off to a staff meeting. Send a note asking if it would be possible to talk to him about your child's reading and ask if he could suggest a convenient time.

2 Think about what you want to say to the teacher beforehand – practise it if you feel nervous! Sometimes writing a list of all the points you want to mention can help.

3 Be tactful and don't be aggressive or lose your temper! (Even if you do feel like it.) ALL of us react badly when we are confronted by an angry person who seems to be attacking us and so nothing very much is likely to be achieved. It's your

child who matters most, so if that means you have to take a deep breath to stay calm then so be it!

Instead of saying something like 'Davy's reading book is much too hard for him and what's more this is the second week he's brought it home, so what are you going to do about it?' try saying something along the lines of:

'I'm rather worried about Davy's reading. He is finding his reading book very hard and for some reason he seems to be bringing the same one home night after night. I'm sure he hasn't said anything to you but I wonder if you could help – perhaps by persuading him to bring an easier book home?'

Putting your complaint in this way still leaves the teacher in no doubt about the problem, but it doesn't attack his professional status, and also gives him a way of sorting things out. This is especially so if the teacher doesn't want to admit that he didn't realise there was a problem – and that can happen all too easily with class sizes the way they are.

The number of parents who experience problems with a school is very small. It is far more likely to be the case that you are satisfied with what the teacher is trying to do. If there should be a problem, however, don't let it slide – talk to the class teacher, or to the headteacher if you think that would be easier.

One of the phrases which is widely used in education these days is 'partnership with parents'. Slowly but surely, schools have begun to realise and appreciate the role that parents have to play with regard to children's education, and most now do their best to encourage parents to be involved.

Your child's school may, for example:

- hold curriculum evenings for parents, where they explain and discuss their various teaching approaches
- have a booklet or leaflet available which advises parents on how best to support their child's reading
- invite parents to come into classrooms and help the teacher by playing games or talking with the children, reading stories to a small group and so on.

All such activities are over and above the open evenings which are set up for parents to discuss their child's progress with the teacher.

Many parents would like to be more involved with their child's school but they cannot – because they are working, because there is a young baby at home and so on. You can,

Children want to share their developing reading skills with their parents.

however, still support your child's reading development at home by:

- sharing the books the school sends home and listening to your child read
- praising and acknowledging your child's growing ability with reading – even if progress is slow
- providing and sharing *other* books at home to extend the reading diet – by belonging to the local library, for example
- continuing to read aloud to your child even though she or he has begun or is reading independently
- asking your child's teacher from time to time if there is anything in particular you could be doing at home to help (ask at an open evening or by sending a note)
- making sure that your child sees you reading. It is very important for children to see the adults they love best using and enjoying their reading skills. It's no good telling a child that reading is important if they never see you doing it! Children learn by example in reading as they do anything else.

SHARING BOOKS AND LISTENING TO CHILDREN READING

Depending on how difficult a book is for your child, there are several ways you can use it together. As a *rough* guide:

- a book that a child is expected to read alone and independently should have no more than about one in every 25 words that he doesn't know or cannot read. More than this means that your child is unlikely to gain maximum understanding of the contents without some support
- where there are about one in every 15 to 20 words which are unfamiliar, your child will need some help to cope. This is about the level of difficulty to expect of a book which is intended for your child to read to you
- where about one in every ten words are unknown, you need to provide greater support. For example: you read parts or the whole thing first and then re-read it together; or you read and your child joins in the parts that he or she can; or you read a sentence and then your child reads it
- where your child only knows approximately every other word in a book then this is one for you to read to your child. You can, of course, always re-read it together if your child wants to join in with any of it.

Listening to your child read at home is probably the most common and effective way for parents to help their children's reading – as long as the book is not too difficult for them. There are certain points to bear in mind to make this time together as effective as possible:

1 Choose a time when you *both* want to read – unwillingness on either side is unlikely to be very helpful!
2 Try to sit comfortably alongside your child in surroundings which are free from distraction – with the television turned off, for example!
3 If it is a new book, look at the cover together, at the title, and ask your child what he thinks the book might be about. Perhaps glance through at the pictures, too. All this is intended to give your child some idea of what the book is about so that reading it is approached with more confidence and ease.

    If the book is one your child has already started reading,

then ask what has happened so far and look at the pictures for reminders. Finish this introduction by asking what your child thinks might happen next.

4 From time to time during the reading at suitable points, ask what might happen next or say: 'I think so and so might do such and such next – what do you think?' Occasionally you can make a wrong or silly prediction so that your child has the fun of being proved right when you were wrong.

5 Depending on your child's preference, take time to look at, comment on and discuss illustrations – either during the reading or at the end. Some children like to linger over illustrations as they go through a book; others prefer to get on with the story. Looking at illustrations afterwards is a good way of recapping on what has been read: 'Do you remember what was happening here?' for example.

6 After the reading, try to check your child's understanding – but do it subtly, not as an interrogation! Try any of the following ways:
   - 'Which bit did you like best? Why was that?'
   - 'Was there anything you didn't like in the story?'
   - 'I can't remember, why did so and so do such and such?'
   - 'Why don't you tell mummy/daddy about the story we've just read?' (Make sure you listen to the retelling to someone else.)
   - 'I wonder how so and so felt when such and such happened?'

7 Always finish off the session on a note of praise and encouragement.

8 The session should last as long as your child's interest holds and no longer. Five minutes of enjoyment and fun are ten times better than ten minutes of a reluctant struggle.

9 If you find yourself losing patience for any reason then STOP. It *is* irritating and frustrating when children cannot read the word they've just read on the previous page (or even the previous line!), for example. But don't let your irritation show and don't let yourself say things like: 'But you must know that word, we've just read it!' Much better to say something like: 'That's the word you read just now, it says *because*.' Only do this if the word is on the same page, point to the word and speak encouragingly, not critically. Remember, if your child *could* read the word, he *would*!

10 Helping your child to deal with unfamiliar words is really the nitty gritty of listening to him read. This is dealt with in some detail in the next section.

If you can't remember the following advice or it seems too complicated, then *simply tell your child what the unknown word is.*

Dealing with unfamiliar words

When we read we are using three lots of information and knowledge:

1 Meaning

This is the meaning within a text but it is also the meaning that we impose on a text; in life we expect things to make sense so we try to make it so when we read. We expect to find meaning in our reading and we try to relate what we read to our own experience and to what we know already.

This is called using *semantic information.*

2 The way language works

We know about the ways words hang together, how you can say certain things but not others. We know, for example, that we don't say: 'The barking dog the door is at.' but we do say: 'The dog is barking at the door.' Like children, most of us cannot say *why* this is so – we just know that one sounds right and the other sounds wrong and we have learned this because we have learned to speak. We bring this understanding of the way language works to our reading.

This is called using *syntactic information.*

3 Sounds to symbols

Language is made up of sounds which make words. We understand that certain patterns of letters are likely to be pronounced in a certain way. You have never seen these words before (because they don't exist) but you could, all the same, pronounce them: *silfew, bonter, articious.*

This is called using *grapho-phonic information.*

We use these three lots of information and knowledge when we are reading to anticipate what the next words might be; but we are not aware of what we are doing until we meet an unfamiliar word. Then we tend to skip over it, read on a little, go back and have another shot and look at parts of the word and puzzle out what they might be. Finally we satisfy ourselves that what we think it is makes sense and we carry on. Reading has been well described as a problem solving activity.

Children in the process of learning to read need to be helped to make use of the three kinds of information and knowledge outlined earlier. However, it is useless telling them about it in the way that I have described it to you! Instead, we help them to use the knowledge and information by the way we prompt or help them when they come to an unknown word. Learning how to read concerns learning how to cope with and work out unfamiliar words. The advice which follows is what teachers do (and should do, because it is the approach recommended in the National Curriculum Programme of Study for Reading).

WHEN YOUR CHILD MAKES A MISTAKE
BUT DOES NOT CORRECT IT:

Encourage your child to correct it for him or herself by saying something like:
- 'Something didn't make sense/sound right there, did it?'
- 'Have another look at this part here.'
- 'Are you sure that's what it says?'

Children will often not correct themselves if the word they have substituted makes sense within the context of what they are reading: saying 'mum' for 'mother', for example.

More often than not children need to read on a few words before they realise that a mistake has been made, so do give your child *time* to self-correct before you intervene, by waiting until the end of a sentence or a 'natural break' in the text.

WHEN A CHILD STOPS BECAUSE A WORD IS UNKNOWN:

1 Prompt by saying something like:
- 'Can you guess what this word might be?'
- 'What would make sense there?'
- 'What would fit in here?'

2 Help your child to guess sensibly by asking things like:
- 'Let's miss it out and read on . . . now can you guess?'
- 'Go back to the beginning of the sentence and have another try.'
- 'How does the word begin? Now can you guess what it could be?'

- 'What do you think the beginning of the word sounds like?'
- 'Look at the picture . . . does that help you guess what the word could be?'

3 Get your child to check the guess by asking:
- 'Does that make sense?'
- 'Does it sound right?'
- 'Does what you said match the look of the word?'

4 Give your child some feedback about what he or she is trying to do. For example:
- 'Yes, that would make sense but it's not the word the writer used. Have another look/ The actual word says . . .'
- 'I like the way you tried to work out what that word says.'
- 'Well done! You realised that something didn't make sense there didn't you?'
- 'Aren't you clever working that bit out like that! Tell me what you tried to do.'
- 'I really like the way you read that – you made it sound really exciting/just the way that real people talk!'

Comments such as this not only boost your child's self-confidence but they give them some insights as to how to tackle difficulties in their reading.

GAMES AND ACTIVITIES FOR LANGUAGE DEVELOPMENT, READING AND WRITING

Which way to the library?

WHAT TO DO

Make a regular visit to the library. On the way talk about the shops you pass. Show your child the signs you pass. Gradually encourage him to tell you which way to go next, at regular intervals on the journey.

Good for:
- encouraging awareness of direction
- introducing the language of direction: eg left and right, straight on, past the Post Office, down the hill.

The print all around us offers wonderful teaching opportunities. Talk about it and encourage your child to notice signs and words in the environment.

What's my name?

YOU WILL NEED:

- to write your child's name on a piece of paper. Use a thick marker and make the letters at least 5 cm high.

WHAT TO DO

Encourage him to trace over the letters with his finger while saying his name.

Then, with your help, ask him to shut his eyes, think of what his name looks like and trace it in the air. This can be followed with attempts to write his name on paper. You are aiming for him to be able to write his whole name from memory without having to check letter for letter.

Encourage him to:
- look at his name written
- cover it up
- write his whole name from memory
- check which letters he has right and then try again.

Cook It

YOU WILL NEED:

- a cookery book, preferably a children's version, such as *The Usborne First Cookbook* by Angela Wilkes and Stephen Cartwright (Usborne). To start, choose a recipe that has only a few ingredients and that does not require actual 'cooking'
- the necessary ingredients.

WHAT TO DO

Follow the instructions in the recipe, allowing your child to do as much as he can by himself. (Obviously, do not allow them to tackle knives or other sharp objects!)

Encourage him to talk about what he is doing as he does it. This is a good time to experience and talk about taste, smell and a feel of the things you are using.

Good for:

- realising that books are a source of information
- measuring
- describing what he is doing and using
- co-ordination
- experiencing the success of making something that he can eat himself.

With practice he will become more independent and require less of your help. Then you might each make up the same recipe and compare the results!

A letter for me and a letter for you

WHAT TO DO

Write simple notes to your child telling him about eg, a trip that is planned, how well he put his toys back in their boxes.

Encourage friends or relatives to write short letters to him that he needs to answer.

At first the letters will be a line of scribbles. If you have shown him the letters you receive, this is probably what they look like to him. When he begins to realise that some words always look the same – eg his name – he may include these. There may be some letters that he can remember to write that are included. Praise him for his efforts.

It is important to encourage and value a young child's pretend writing – it makes them want to continue learning to write.

At this stage the most beneficial thing for you to do is to ask him to read his letter to you. When he has finished, praise him for any new features that look like words or letters that he has included.

It is always a temptation to write down your child's ideas for him without giving him the opportunity to try by himself first. If he is used to trying things out without fear of mistakes he is more likely to quickly become a confident, independent writer. It is better to let him try and to provide him with any words or letters he wants, than to always write everything for him first and so make him dependent on you.

Good for:

- understanding that messages aren't only found in books and on signs
- realising that his 'writing' can carry a message to someone else.

My own book

YOU WILL NEED:
- a few sheets of A4 paper, folded in half to make book
- a sheet of coloured A4 card for the cover
- crayons.

WHAT TO DO

Talk about an interesting incident (birthday, Christmas) or trip out. Encourage your child to think of the best parts of the experience and draw a picture for each.

Ask him to think up what message can be added to the drawings for other people to read. Add souvenirs, eg tickets, photographs.

Add his own book to his book collection for reading.
Good for:
- linking spoken and written messages
- using memory of incidents and feelings linked with them
- satisfaction of producing something of his own.

Home-made books are an excellent way of encouraging writing. They are also fun to look back on in later years.

75

And finally . . . don't forget . . .

Keep talking and listening to your child and link what you say with what you are both doing. Include planning and thinking things through as part of a daily routine for your child, as well as for you.

Practise what you preach. For example, if you want to get over the message that you value reading or writing, the best way to make that impression on your child is to read and write for yourself when he is around.

LEARNING ABOUT LETTERS

Letters are the building blocks of written language and represent an important aspect of learning for young children. They have to learn letter names, sounds, their order in the alphabet and how to form them correctly. Children should NOT, however, be expected to learn the different aspects all at once!

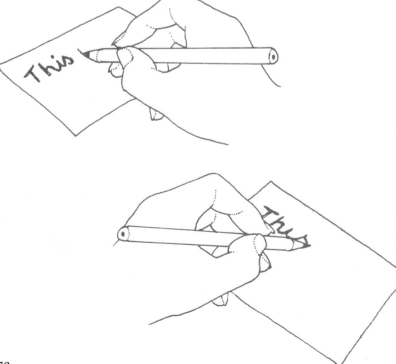

These are the pencil grips for right-handed (top) and left-handed (bottom) people which you should try and encourage your child to use.

Letter formation

Being able to form letters correctly or conventionally is vital if children are to develop good handwriting later on. In the first instance, all children should acquire the control that is necessary to form letter shapes by lots of scribbling, drawing and pattern-making activities. When they can control a pencil or crayon and make it do what they want it to do, they are ready to begin to form letters. Many children have started to do this with their parents' help before they are five.

If you are helping or are going to help your child to form letters, then there are some important things to note:

1 See if you can encourage your child to hold the pencil correctly in the way shown in the illustration. If your child is left-handed then he should be encouraged to tilt the paper away from the left hand and down towards the right at an angle of about 45 degrees. This makes it easier for a child to see the marks he is making without adopting a 'hooked' or 'claw' hand position. Left-handed children often curl their writing hand around over the top of their writing in an effort to stop the hand masking what they write; this is not very comfortable, especially later on when children have to write a lot.

2 Please don't teach your child to write in capital letters: eg CHRISTOPHER HAS A PET RABBIT. Always teach and use the lower case or 'small' letter form – except, of course, where a capital is usual – like at the start of a sentence or a name.

3 If at all possible, check with the school what style of writing they teach.

Some schools use what is called a 'ball and stick' style of printing, and others teach a style where a tail, flick or serif is added to all letters which end in a downward stroke. There may be slight variations with individual letters but, essentially, the two styles are as shown. The starting point and direction have been added to each letter to make it easier for you to teach correctly.

If you do not know which style your child's school teaches, go for the second one. This style makes it easier to learn joined handwriting later on.

The two basic letter styles to choose from.

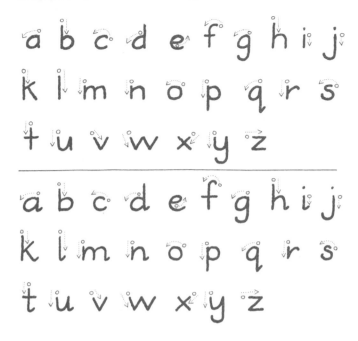

Letter sounds

Teachers help children to learn the most commonly used letter sounds to begin with, so it would be best if you were to do this too.

a as in ambulance	**b** as in boy	**c** as in cat
d as in dad	**e** as in elephant	**f** as in fish
g as in girl	**h** as in house	**i** as in indian
j as in jelly	**k** as in kettle	**l** as in ladder
m as in mum	**n** as in nest	**o** as in octopus
p as in parrot	**q** as in queen	**r** as in rabbit
s as in sun	**t** as in tap	**u** as in umbrella
v as in van	**w** as in window	**x** as in fox
y as in yellow	**z** as in zip	

The best way of referring to letters is to say something like: 'This is m (name) and it usually says mmmm like in mummmm.'

One of the most common ways of teaching children about letter sounds as well as letter names and alphabetical order is through the use of ABC books and alphabet friezes. There are several excellent ABC books and friezes available in the shops. Go for ones which have interesting pictures that represent objects or activities your child is likely to be familiar with. (See page 50 for suggestions for Alphabet books.)

You can, of course, make your own alphabet friezes or books (in a scrapbook, perhaps?) using family photographs, pictures cut from magazines or wrapping paper, your child's or members of the family's drawings or even, for friezes, objects fixed in place. Whether it is a book or a frieze you make, write both forms of the letter and the name of the object/person: eg R r Robert's red rabbit. Put the letters at top left of the space or page and the name under the photograph or picture.

Two games for learning letter sounds

I spy with my little eye . . .

Although this game has been around for a long time it is still a source of much enjoyment – once children understand what they have to do!

Find an object in view that your child knows and say: 'I spy with my little eye something beginning with . . .'. Then give the sound at the beginning of the word: eg mmm for mat or sl for slipper.

At first you will have to give your child the answer, showing the chosen object at the same time. Limit the things looked for to a few beginning with the same sound: eg b for ball, baby or book. Get your child to join in and eventually supply the answer. Once he understands what to do you can branch out to include words beginning with another letter sound. Then introduce more and more sounds gradually.

Sounds and pictures

TO MAKE:

Copy or trace the pictures on page 81 on to plain paper or card and cut them into separate squares. Using another piece of paper or card cut 25 separate pieces to match the picture cards in size. Write one letter of the alphabet on each card, excluding x.

TO PLAY:

Do not introduce all the letters at once; select four or five with sounds that are not easily confused – m s j a k, for example.

Check that your child knows what the selected pictures represent and show how each one has an accompanying letter: eg 'moon ... mmmmoon ... and here's the letter at the beginning of the word, mmm'.

STAGE 1:

Randomly spread your chosen pictures and letters on the table and then see if your child can join in with you in matching any pictures and letters.

STAGE 2:

See if your child can do it without your help.

STAGE 3:

Gradually introduce more pictures and letters by repeating the steps outlined above.

A more advanced game

STAGE 1:

Spread out some of the pictures and their letters face down on the table and shuffle them around.

Turn over two of the cards and see if they match: eg w and window. If they do, remove the pair and place to one side. If they do not match, replace the cards as they were and try again. The object is to collect pairs by gradually remembering where the various cards are.

STAGE 2:

Take it in turns to turn over the cards in pairs.

STAGE 3:

Play with all the cards. Very challenging!

Illustrations to copy for making the letter sounds game (see page 79).

BOOKS FOR BEGINNER READERS: AGES 5–7

When children are just beginning to learn to read, the following features will help to make it an easy and enjoyable process:

- a limited amount of text on each page
- clear print of a reasonable size
- repeated phrases
- sentences that are easy to predict because they follow the same pattern
- rhythmical and/or rhyming words
- language with which they are familiar
- a good story

Look out for these things when you are choosing books for your child. All the books in the following list have some or all of these features. They are also all books which bear re-reading many times – the acid test for books for beginner readers. It goes without saying that if you read the book through together once or twice before your child tries alone, you will be making the task of reading even easier. It also goes without saying that your child may start to learn to read on any of his old favourites, memorised and loved over the years.

All children are individuals and each will have their own time, place and book to start on; it could be a recipe book, a comic or a newspaper! Also, many of the books in the previous list (on pages 44–52) will be suitable as books for beginning readers.

Whatever books your child is learning to read with at school, you will be helping even more if you provide more reading material at home, be it children's picture books, comics, newspapers or whatever your child wants to read. Never think you may be interfering or doing the wrong thing – you cannot provide too wide a diet for your bookworm.

Note: The books in this list range in difficulty from those with very simple and few words for absolute beginners to more text and more difficult language for those gaining the skills and needing to practise them. It is also worth remembering that books with very few words may not necessarily be easy to read.

Ahhh! Said Stork *Gerald Rose*
  Macmillan 1986
Each of the animals tries a different way to crack the egg. One short sentence per page and helpful clues from the pictures.

Bears In The Night *Stan & Jan Berenstain*
  Collins 1972
The Berenstain bears jump out of bed and venture up Spook Hill. They get such a fright that they rush all the way home and end up safely back in bed. Once confident, children love to read this faster and faster – especially on the return journey. For absolute beginners. Another popular book about the Berenstain bears, with a little more text, is **The Spooky Old Tree**.

The Bear's Toothache *David McPhail*
  Magnet 1984
A delightful tale of a little boy who causes chaos in the house one night as he tries to get rid of the bear's aching tooth.

Big Dog ... Little Dog *P. D. Eastman*
  Picture Lion 1973
An easy-to-read story about two doggy friends, Fred and Ted, who go for a holiday in the mountains and have trouble sleeping ... until they find the perfect solution ...

But Martin! *June Counsel*
  Picture Corgi 1986
A day in the life of four children at primary school who meet Martin the Martian. A book about tolerating others.

Bringing The Rain To Kapiti Plain *Verna Aardema*
Picturemac 1986
A traditional African folk tale told in the style of 'This is the house that Jack built'. This makes for a rhythmical and repetitive read so important for a beginner reader. The wide African landscapes are drawn by Beatriz Vidal.

Cat On The Mat   *Brian Wildsmith*
OUP 1982
An expanded version of 'The cat sat on the mat'. Lots of other animals sit on it, too, until it gets rather overcrowded. One in a series of brightly coloured, inexpensive books for complete beginners. Other titles to try: **My Dream**; **Giddy Up**; **The Island** and **All Fall Down**.

Don't Forget The Bacon! *Pat Hutchins*
Picture Puffin 1978
A boy is sent to the shops with a list of things to remember. As he repeats it to himself, the list changes a bit on each page and he buys some very odd things. Everything ends up all right in the end but of course he does forget the bacon. Visual clues on each page will help the beginner read what the boy is thinking.

The Fat Cat *Jack Kent*
Picture Puffin 1974
This amusing Danish folk tale is about a cat who gets fatter and fatter as he eats everything in his path until he meets the woodcutter.

Funny Bones *Janet & Allan Ahlberg*
Picture Lion 1982
One dark, dark night a family of skeletons go for a walk to frighten someone . . . and end up frightening each other.

Goodnight, Owl! *Pat Hutchins*
Picture Puffin 1975
Owl cannot sleep in the daytime because the other birds keep him awake. But he gets his own back when night falls.

Happy Families *Allan Ahlberg*
Puffin 1980/88
Allan Ahlberg has the rare knack of knowing what makes children laugh and has created in these 16 little books stories which will keep them giggling while they read. Favourites include: **Mrs Wobble The Waitress**; **Mrs Lather's Laundry**; **Mr Tick The Teacher** and **Miss Brick The Builder's Baby**.

Have You Seen My Cat? *Eric Carle*
Picture Knight 1989
A boy who has lost his cat goes round the world looking for it. A very simple repeated text.

I Can Read Books
Heinemann
This series is ideal for children who are just getting the hang of reading and who can cope with a little more text. Each book is a collection of short stories so that not too much need be read at a time. They are the perfect vehicle for developing stamina and fluency and will encourage children to feel: 'I can read!' Outstanding titles in the series are:

Frog And Toad Are Friends; **Frog And Toad All Year**; **Frog And Toad Together**; **Days With Frog And Toad** *Arnold Lobel*
1983
Four collections of gently humorous and warm stories about two very good friends.

Little Bear *Else Holmelund Minarik*
1977
Four short stories about an engaging little bear who has all sorts of adventures under the watchful eye of his loving mother. Also **Father Bear Comes Home**; **Little Bear's Visit**.

Mouse Tales *Arnold Lobel*
   1977
Papa bear tells the little bears seven bedtime stories.
Also: **Mouse Soup**.

Oink And Pearl *Kay Charao*
   1985
Four delightful, funny stories about two little pigs.
Pearl experiences all the difficulties of being the
oldest and only having a boring baby to play with.

King Henry's Palace; The Tale of Thomas Mead
Pat Hutchins
   Young Piper 1988
Three short, simple stories about kind King Henry. Flip
the book over and start again and read the rhyming
cautionary tale of Thomas Mead who couldn't read.

Lend Me Your Wings *John Agard*
   Picture Knight 1988
'On a happy crick-crack morning when wind gives
leaves a small shiver . . .'; so starts the tale of Sister
Fish and Brother Bird who want to change places.
Wonderfully vibrant storytelling.

Lily Takes A Walk *Satoshi Kitamura*
   Picture Corgi 1988
Lily goes for a walk through the town with her dog,
Nicky. She is not afraid because she has Nicky with
her but she doesn't see what Nicky and we can see
behind her.

Meg And Mog Books *Helen Nicoll & Jan Pienkowski*
   Picture Puffin 1975
These books about a witch called Meg, her cat Mog and
Owl are deservedly popular with beginner readers. The
format is designed to appeal: large words on brightly
coloured background, big bold pictures and busy
layouts. Best of the series: **Meg and Mog**; **Meg's Eggs**;
Meg On The Moon; **Meg's Castle** and **Mog At The
Zoo**.

**Monster And The Baby; Monster Can't Sleep;
Monster And The Playhouse; A Halloween Mask For
Monster** *Virginia Mueller*
   Picture Puffin 1988
Children will love this adorable, toothy little green
monster in situations familiar to them. Very simple,
short sentences make these a delightful set of first books
for learning to read pleasurably.

Mister Magnolia *Quentin Blake*
   Picture Lion 1981
He is very fortunate in all sorts of ways, BUT . . . Mr
Magnolia has only one boot! The rhyme, rhythm and
sense of humour make this a winner for beginner
readers. A rewarding experience to share it together
first.

Noisy Nora *Rosemary Wells*
   Picture Lion 1978
Nora, the middle mouse in the family, feels left out
while Mum and Dad are busy with her brother and
sister. A rhyming story which is a great pleasure to
read rhythmically in a sing-song way.

Not Like That, Like This! *Tony Bradman & Joanna
Burroughes*
   Beaver 1990
When Dad gets his head stuck fast in the park railings,
more and more people come to his aid, but to no avail
until, finally, the fire brigade manages it. A super book
for counting the helpers and chanting the repeated
phrases.

Not Now, Bernard *David McKee*
   Sparrow 1980
Another story about a child who feels ignored. Bernard
is eaten by a monster who is also ignored by Bernard's
mother and father! Children love droning the repeated
phrase 'Not now, Bernard'.

The Paper Bag Princess *Robert N. Munsch*
   Hippo 1982
A feminist fairytale. Elizabeth uses her brains to outwit
the dragon and rescue Prince Ronald, only to decide
that she would rather not marry him after all.

Reading Time
   Walker
Walker have reissued some of their picture books
(including some of the Red Nose Readers mentioned
here) in this new series, in which the books are colour-
coded into levels of difficulty as a guide to parents: first
words, repetition, dialogue, rhyme, first story books.

Bet You Can't *Penny Dale*
   Walker Reading Time 1990
A black brother and sister quarrel over who's best at
what while tidying their room but end up the best of
friends. Very simply told in speech bubbles.

Red Nose Readers *Allan Ahlberg & Colin McNaughton*
Walker 1985
Although called 'Readers', these little books have nothing in common with school reading books except that they are 'graded' into three levels: Red for one, two or three word-phrases; Yellow for short sentences; and Blue for rhymes. All the books are funny, jokily illustrated and definitely make learning to read FUN!

This Is The Bear *Sarah Hayes*
Walker Reading Time 1990
A rhyming story about a lost teddy. Very simple. Also: **This Is The Bear And The Picnic Lunch**.

Snowball Books:
Kittens In The Kitchen; Hamster In Hiding; Goat In The Garden; Puppy In The Park *Helen Piers*
Magnet 1984
Four animal story books with superb photographs. Each story builds up with repeated phrases.

The Straw Maid *Anita Lobel*
Hippo 1984
A traditional tale about a girl who is captured by robbers and escapes by playing a trick on them.

Teeny Tiny *Jill Bennett*
OUP 1987
The best version of this old tale of the 'teeny tiny woman' who 'takes a teeny tiny walk' and finds a 'teeny tiny bone'. The constant repetition makes for an easy read.

The Tiny Tiny Tadpole *H. E. Todd*
Picture Corgi 1987
An amusing and informative look at the life cycle of a frog. Not for absolute beginners: more suitable for the top of this age range. Also: **The Crawly Crawly Caterpillar**.

The Trouble With Mum *Babette Cole*
Picture Lion 1985
What makes this book work so well is the mismatch between the words and the pictures: eg underneath a picture of mum, in witch's clothes and turning the parents at the PTA meeting into frogs, is written: 'She didn't seem to get on with the other parents.'

Witches Four *Marc Brown*
Picture Corgi 1985
A simply rhyming story about four witches who lose their hats.

Would You Rather . . . *John Burningham*
Picture Lion 1984
Bizarre alternatives from which to choose: eg 'Would you rather . . . jump in the nettles for £5, swallow a dead frog for £20 or stay all night in a creepy house for £50?' Will delight every childish sense of humour.

Books to read with your child

These are books for you to read with your child sitting beside you so that you can look at the pictures together and discuss the story as you read. On the whole the length and difficulty of the text makes them most suitable for an adult to read at this stage but your child may want to join in with some of the reading as well.

Babylon *Jill Paton Walsh*
Beaver 1985
In the middle of the dismal city streets, three Afro-Caribbean children discover a Hanging Gardens of Babylon on top of the old viaduct.

Burglar Bill *Janet & Allan Ahlberg*
Little Mammoth 1989
Burglar Bill's life is changed when he finds a baby and takes it home. Huge fun.

Cat And Canary *Michael Foreman*
Picture Knight 1989
With the aid of a kite, Cat flies high over the city with his friend, Canary, and is back in time for tea.

Fred *Posy Simmonds*
Picture Puffin 1989
Sophie and Nick are very sad when their cat, Fred, dies, until they discover that he was the most famous cat in the world. The full-colour comic-strip format also appeals to older children.

Jamaica's Find *Juanita Havill*
   Little Mammoth 1990
Jamaica finds an old toy dog in the park and takes it
home to keep. After some thought she decides to take
it back and find its rightful owner. A well-told, thought-
provoking tale. Illustrated by Anne Sibley O'Brien.

The Giant Jam Sandwich *John Vernon Lord & Janet
Burroway*
   Piccolo 1974
The story, told in verse, of how the villagers of Itching
Down get rid of a plague of wasps.

Gorilla *Anthony Browne*
   Magnet 1985
Hannah lives with her father who is too busy to take
her to the zoo. On the eve of her birthday she has an
amazing adventure with her new toy gorilla and her
birthday turns out to be the happiest ever.

The Jolly Postman *Janet & Allan Ahlberg*
   Heinemann 1986
A really inventive book containing letters, circulars,
postcards, birthday cards etc to storybook characters.
You can take them out of their envelopes to read.

The King Bird *A. H. Benjamin*
   Picture Corgi 1989
A very funny story about a king who loves birds and
his wife who doesn't. Illustrated by Tony Ross.

The Little Peacock's Gift A Chinese folk tale retold
Illustrated by Cherry Denham
   Picture Corgi 1990
By doing good to others, the smallest peacock
eventually becomes the one chosen to learn the
peacock fairy's secrets. Superb illustrations.

Little Red Riding Hood *Tony Ross*
   Picture Puffin 1981
A wittily original version of this traditional tale. For
more of Tony Ross's wickedly funny retellings in Picture
Puffins see **Lazy Jack** and **Foxy Fables**.

Patch The Pirate Cat *Andrew Martyr*
   Picture Corgi 1989
A romp round the pirates' ship as Captain Blackeye
Finnegan and his crew chase Patch to catch him for a
bath. Tremendous fun.

Sixes And Sevens *John Yeoman*
   Picturemac 1988
Barnaby sails up the river on his raft, collecting
stranger and stranger items to deliver at Limber Lea.
A romp of a counting book, with zany drawings by
Quentin Blake.

The Teddy Robber *Ian Beck*
   Doubleday 1989 Hardback
A beautifully illustrated book for teddy bear owners
whatever their age!

What-a-Mess Goes To School *Frank Muir*
   Picture Corgi 1987
What-a-Mess, the Afghan puppy, is hopeless at dog
training school. All he gets is minus marks and he
despairs of passing his final test until Cynthia the
hedgehog comes to the rescue. The best of the **What-
a-Mess** books.

The Winter Bear *Ruth Craft*
   Picture Lion 1976
Three children go for a walk in the country and find a
lost teddy. Delicate, wintry pictures by Eric Blegvad.

Books to read to your child: ages 5–7

When children are learning to read for
themselves it is still essential that you
continue to read *to* them. They will not want
a diet of simple stories alone and will
appreciate the opportunity to *hear* the richer
language and longer, more complicated plots
that you can read to them. This will also
prepare them for the sort of language they
will meet in the future when they are able to
tackle more advanced books. It is also
important at this stage to provide time to
relax from the effort of learning to read and
to sit back and enjoy entering other worlds
created by someone else.

Bimwili And The Zimwi *Verna Aardema*
   Picturemac 1988
A tale from Zanzibar. The Zimwi catches Bimwili and
puts her in his drum to sing for his supper.

Cinderella *Charles Perrault*
   Picture Puffin 1976
The classic version of this much-loved fairy story. The
language is quite advanced but it is beautifully
illustrated by Errol Le Cain.

The Clothes Horse *Janet & Allan Ahlberg*
   Puffin 1989
Six pieces of Ahlberg whimsy which interpret common
phrases literally.

A Dragon In Class 4 *June Counsel*
   Young Corgi 1986
A real dragon called Scales decides to join Class 4. He
is Sam's special friend and helps him with his reading
and spelling.

Do Goldfish Play The Violin? *David Henry Wilson*
   Piper 1988
Hilarious stories about life as seen through the eyes of
the irrepressible Jeremy James. Parents and children
will roar with laughter as he causes embarrassment,
bewilderment and mayhem. For other adventures with
Jeremy James see: **Elephants Don't Sit On Cars**;
Getting Rich With Jeremy James; **Beside The Sea
With Jeremy James** and **How To Stop A Train With
One Finger**.

Fantastic Mr Fox *Roald Dahl*
   Young Puffin 1974
In this story the fox is the hero and children will cheer
him on in his battle for survival against his enemies,
Farmers Boggis, Bunce and Bean. Fluent readers of this
age will enjoy tackling this for themselves.

A Necklace Of Raindrops *Joan Aiken*
   Puffin 1974
Magical stories, some in modern settings, some a long
time ago. Superbly written with black and white
silhouettes by Jan Pienkowski.

Our Sleepysaurus *Martin Waddell*
   Walker Read Aloud 1989
Three stories about Marigold, Rashid and Niki who
have a secret pet with an enormous appetite.

The Owl Who Was Afraid Of The Dark *Jill
Tomlinson*
   Young Puffin 1973
Plop is a baby barn owl who is afraid of the dark. His
mother sends him out into the world to talk to people
who think differently.

Ponders *Russell Hoban*
   Walker Read Aloud 1989
Eight stories about the creatures who live in and
around a country pond.

The Puffin Book Of Animal Stories *Anita Hewett*
   Puffin 1988
Packed with stories from around the world and perfect
for that rainy afternoon, ride in the car or bedtime.

Stories For Six-Year-Olds *Edited by Sara & Stephen
Corrin*
   Puffin 1976
A collection of mainly traditional tales from England
and other parts of the world. Also: **Stories For Five-
Year-Olds**; **Stories For Seven-Year-Olds**; **More
Stories For Seven-Year-Olds** etc.

Read and Listen Series *Various authors*
   BBC Books/Longman 1990
A colourful and appealing variety of stories and poems;
two audiocassettes accompany the first six books in
which well-known actors bring the stories alive.

Poetry for 5–7s

Poetry speaks personally to all children and many come to love reading through it. Reading aloud rhymes, nonsense and funny and rhythmical verse is a good introduction to poetry at this age.

Inky Pinky Ponky *Collected by Michael Rosen & Susanna Steele*
    Picture Lion 1989
Playground rhymes to savour on the tongue. With bright, busy pictures by Dan Jones.

Mother Goose Comes To Cable Street *Chosen by Rosemary Stones & Andrew Mann*
    Picture Puffin 1980
This collection of nursery rhymes is brought up to date for modern children with (again) Dan Jones' bright detailed paintings of children in today's multi-ethnic, inner-city London.

Once Upon A Rhyme *Sarah & Stephen Corrin*
    Young Puffin 1984
101 poems to read to 5–7s including A. A. Milne, Spike Milligan, James Reeves, John Keats, Edward Lear and many more.

Roger Was A Razor Fish *Compiled by Jill Bennett*
    Hippo 1983
A delightful collection of short poems which young children will love to join in and learn by heart or read for themselves.

Say It Again, Granny! *John Agard*
    Magnet 1987
As it says on the cover, this has 'Twenty poems from Caribbean Proverbs'. Also: **I Din Do Nuttin**.

The Young Puffin Book Of Verse *Compiled by Barbara Ireson*
    Young Puffin 1970
Great to read aloud and packed with all sorts of treats. The book is divided into sections on different themes: eg Out of Doors; All the Animals; One Two Three.

First word books and dictionaries

The following examples range from early word books arranged in topic order and simple picture dictionaries (both suitable for browsing through and for word finding for writing) to dictionaries suitable for the top primary aged child who wants a handy reference for looking up spellings and meanings of words.

Breakthrough Dictionary
    Longman 1984 Hardback
2000 entries in alphabetical order within 30 topics. (5–7 years.)

My First Animal Word Book *Edwina Riddell*
    Frances Lincoln 1989
Each page of this book is covered with detailed illustrations of animals which are clearly labelled. Good for word recognition for beginner readers and useful as an introduction to finding words for writing.

Collins Picture Dictionary
    Collins 1989 Hardback
Not in alphabetical order, but in topics: eg At the Seaside; Doctors and Dentists. It has pictures with lots of labels on them and some definitions are given. Useful for spelling.

The Oxford Children's Dictionary
    OUP 1985
Pocket-sized paperback with 12000 entries and concise, accurate definitions. Some pictures. (Nearly adult.)

The Oxford Illustrated Junior Dictionary
    OUP 1989 Hardback
An excellent first proper dictionary. The entries are written in red and the meanings in black. The definitions are clear and simple. It tells us there are 5000 entries and 300 pictures. Hardback.

The Young Person's Picture Dictionary
    Oliver & Boyd 1990
Clear, uncluttered layout with simple, chatty definitions and examples. (5–7 years.)

3 MOVING ON WITH READING:
ages 7+

Children have learned a great deal in the years from birth to seven. They have learned to talk, they have been introduced to the world of books and they have begun to read quite well for themselves. In the junior years they build on what they have learned so far. The world of books becomes more accessible to them and all kinds of exciting highways and byways open up in front of them.

In this part of the book we look at reading in school in the junior years and at how you can encourage reading at home. We also suggest some questions you can ask yourself about your child's reading development.

Many journeys are possible in the world of books....

Most children's reading skills *are* developing nicely by seven, although the rate varies enormously from child to child. Some children, however, do face problems with literacy, so at the end of this section we look at children with special needs. Not only does it include children with reading or spelling problems, it also looks at how special needs such as hearing or visual impairment may affect reading.

WHAT YOU CAN DO TO ENCOURAGE THE READING HABIT

There are three important things here: books, time and you!

Make sure your child has access to books

Books are expensive items, as we all know. All children, however, benefit from having some books of their own. Apart from having a book as a birthday or Christmas present, your child may well be able to buy books from school. Many primary schools operate bookshops; frequently they also have a savings scheme to help children who wish to save a small amount of their pocket money each week until they have sufficient to buy a book. This is an idea you might like to copy at home. Encourage your child to make or decorate a small box, label it *Book Box* and put a little of their pocket money in each week. This can be for new books or second-hand ones from jumble sales, for example.

Public libraries are the major source of book provision for children and parents. Even very small or mobile libraries have children's sections and the librarians are always very happy to advise you or your child on suitability and likely appeal of books. They can also be very helpful in recommending information books that your child could use when he is working on a topic or project.

Some parents organise the occasional book swap amongst their children's circles of friends and their brothers and sisters. This can be quite fun:

- invite children to attend at a certain time and, best of all, get your own child to make or help to make invitations
- ask guests to bring at least two or three books they no longer want (suggest that they check with their parents first!)

Book swaps are an effective and cheap way of getting more books.

come to a
BOOK SWAP
at Jamie's house
at 43,
Englewood Way
on Tues. March 6th
at 7.30 p.m.
Bring at least 2
books you don't
want any more!

90

- provide the odd drink/snack
- clear the floor, spread out the books as they arrive and let the children dive in! You may wish to place an initial limit on the number of books any one child can take. It depends how many turn up in the first place!

Make sure your child has time to read

Some children create their own reading time; others need to be encouraged! Many parents find a solution is to say to their children that, at bedtime, they can stay in bed with the lights on so long as they are reading; otherwise it's lights out immediately!

Many children enjoy having their own bedtime reading record on the wall. This can be a large sheet of paper, decorated around the edges by your child, on which he writes

It is important for children not only to have time to read by themselves but also to see their parents reading too.

91

down the titles of books which have been read. It can be very satisfying and motivating to watch the space filling up!

Quite a few families enjoy a family reading time. This is a set few minutes in the evening when everyone reads. This can be individual reading of books, comics, newspapers, magazines etc, according to adults' and children's tastes. It can also be the reading and serialisation of one book (provided your children's age range isn't too wide). Please don't think that books written for children can only be enjoyed by children! Try *Woof!* by Allan Ahlberg, *The BFG* by Roald Dahl or *Goodnight Mister Tom* by Michelle Magorian (all Puffins) as three excellent examples – the first two very funny and entertaining, the second serious but enthralling.

Make sure your child sees YOU reading!

Having a family reading time encourages and provides the opportunity for your child to read and enjoy books. It has the equally important benefit of showing your child that *you* value and enjoy reading too. Parents are powerful role models – in this as in other things children learn by example. Try to involve your child in various kinds of reading activity: checking in the newspaper what's on TV, following a recipe or instructions for DIY, looking out for road signs when travelling, using information books to answer the questions your child asks to which you don't know the answers, and so on. If you use print in any way at all (and we all do to some degree) try your best to encourage your child to share it with you – even though this *is* time-consuming!

READING IN THE JUNIOR SCHOOL

It is likely that children who are in a combined infant and junior school will be receiving a similar approach to the teaching of reading in the early junior years to the one they received in the infants'. Where children transfer to a separate junior school they may also face a change of approach – a different reading scheme, no reading scheme or whatever.

In general terms, however, the reading experiences of the junior years build on foundations laid at infant level. Children should be reading a wider range of fiction and more demanding stories as their reading skills develop further. But learning to read and reading does not simply mean fiction. It also means learning how to select and use books as information sources.

At this point let's consider some of the National Curriculum Attainment Target (AT) requirements at Key Stage 2, which is for seven to eleven-year-olds. (Level Four is the level which most children are expected to attain by the age of eleven.) The following extracts are taken from *English in the National Curriculum* and are reproduced with the permission of the Controller of Her Majesty's Stationery Office.

AT 2 – Reading:

'The development of the ability to read, understand and respond to all types of writing, as well as the development of information-retrieval strategies for the purpose of study'
'Pupils should be able to:

Level Three:

- read aloud from familiar stories and poems fluently and with appropriate expression
- read silently and with sustained concentration
- listen attentively to stories, talk about setting, storyline and characters and recall significant details
- demonstrate, in talking about stories and poems, that they are beginning to use inference, deduction and previous reading experience to find and appreciate meanings beyond the literal
- bring to their writing and discussion about stories some understanding of the way stories are structured
- devise a clear set of questions that will enable them to select and use appropriate information sources and reference books from the class and school library.

Level Four:

- read aloud expressively, fluently and with increased confidence from a range of familiar literature
- demonstrate, in talking about a range of fiction and poetry which they have read, an ability to explore preferences
- demonstrate, in talking about stories and poems, that they are developing their abilities to use inference, deduction and previous reading experience
- find books or magazines in the class or school library by using the classification system, catalogue or data base and

use appropriate methods of finding information, when pursuing a line of enquiry.'

Many of the skills of reading and writing will continue to be developed as they were in the infant years by what is described as a cross-curricular approach. Instead of having a series of separate subjects to study, children work on topics or projects. Teachers plan the topic to bring in areas of study, developing skills and Attainment Target coverage from science, maths and history, for example, as well as English. Topics are broad-based, such as Transport or Communication, to allow for individual children or groups of children to study certain aspects and then share their findings with the class.

Much of the time in class is spent working in small groups or as individuals.

Working in a topic or project-based way does not mean, however, that no actual teaching of important skills such as spelling goes on! Children do not spend *all* their time doing topic work. There is still time for reading for pleasure, for writing creatively and spontaneously, and for developing in all curriculum areas including personal and social skills.

Reading widely is an important aspect of the junior years.

Central to the idea of topic work is the need for children to acquire what are described as the 'reading for learning skills' – to learn to use reading as a means of researching or finding out information. In order to do this children need to be able to:

- identify their purpose for reading: eg reading carefully and accurately in order to answer a question they have set themselves or which has been set for them
- use the library by understanding how it is organised and so be able to find books on particular subjects
- make use of title, list of contents, an index etc, in order to determine whether or not a particular book is likely to be of use for their purpose
- absorb, make notes about and reorganise what they read in order to write about something without copying word for word from the book.

These are difficult skills to learn and while some of the ideas may have been introduced at infant level, the junior years are the time when the greatest development happens. It is worth pointing out that these and similar skills go on developing, being refined and extended in the secondary years too. A child does not learn everything there is to know about reading in the primary years alone!

In the early junior years children need to build up their reading stamina, gradually moving from the short, plentifully illustrated books that most five and six-year-olds read, to the longer children's novel. This does *not* mean that children who are seven plus or even nine plus should not read short picture books. Some short picture books are actually very demanding in terms of their language and their ideas. What it means is that children should have variety in their reading which will include more and more longer books as their age and reading stamina increase.

Children at seven to nine still need help and support in dealing with the technicalities of reading – coping with more complex and demanding words, more sophisticated use of punctuation and so on. They also need help in understanding and appreciating the more complex, sophisticated and demanding stories which they will be reading.

It is quite likely that some group reading will go on in school where a group of children read the same book individually or

Sharing and talking about books in a small group heightens children's understanding, awareness and appreciation – it's also fun!

together. They will then discuss it in some detail, exchanging their views, understandings and interpretations. Whether or not group reading is used, teachers devise various activities which are intended to enhance children's appreciation of a book. These might include role-play or acting out part of a story, pretending to interview characters about their feelings and actions, doing exercises where some of the words have been deleted from an extract from the story which children then fill in, answering questions, making a story into a radio play, rewriting a story from another point of view and so on. Teachers arrange for children to have different types of reading experiences using different types of text. Some examples might be:

96

- reading instructions – to make a model or cook something, for instance
- reading poetry of different kinds – ballads, limericks etc
- reading descriptions
- reading different styles and types of fiction
- reading non-fiction books
- reading plays
- using encyclopedias, dictionaries, reference material, a thesaurus
- listening to and discussing things which other people read aloud.

The junior years are a time of great growth in reading terms!

Supporting the work of the school

Every school realises the need to have up-to-date and extensive book stocks. By no means, however, is every school able to provide the range, quality and number of books that it would wish to have available. It is a matter of money. Your child may well attend a school where you are disappointed in the provision of books. If this is the case it becomes even more important for you to try to ensure that your child gets plenty of additional reading experiences at home – more than parents might usually offer. Your local library should be the best source.

In the junior years try to:
- arrange a variety of books for your child to read at home, including information books, poetry (and comics!)
- continue to read aloud to your child, especially books which he would enjoy but which may be too difficult or daunting to try alone – see page 107 for suggestions
- talk to your child about what he is reading and try to find some time to browse around the library and bookshops with your child
- remember that your child will still need help with reading. Continue to encourage him to deal with unfamiliar words in the way outlined on pages 69–71 when you are listening to him reading.

MONITORING YOUR CHILD'S PROGRESS

There are two ways in which you will be monitoring your child's progress in reading: through your own observations of what he is doing at home and by way of information from the school.

Information from school

Schools are continually monitoring children's progress. They have always done this but further arrangements are being brought in which link with the National Curriculum. All children in England and Wales in state schools will be tested at ages seven, eleven, fourteen and sixteen (as will, in all probability, children in Scotland and Northern Ireland). Children will be assessed as to their levels of attainment within the National Curriculum in two ways. The first is by teachers' judgements and observations relating to the work children have done and the knowledge and skills they possess. The second will be national assessment using Standard Assessment Tasks (SATs). These will not be traditional tests as such; rather, a special project or a series of activities will be set for children to carry out under normal classroom circumstances.

Schools will have to publish their results for eleven, fourteen and sixteen-year-olds. This does not mean individual children's results, but those of the year group as a whole. It is not compulsory for seven-year-olds' results to be published – schools may choose whether or not they will do so. Schools have a duty to pass on information about your child's results to you, but are not allowed to discuss any other individual child's results with you.

Children will be assessed at other times as well as the reporting ages of seven and eleven. Teachers are continually observing and checking what children can do in order to plan the next phase of work. Information along these lines will be passed on to you at parents' evenings or in reports.

Parents' evenings are a good time to ask questions about your child's reading. The teacher will tell you if things are coming along as they should, whether or not your child needs some extra reading teaching, whether or not and how you can help to extend your child's reading and so on.

Your observations

In general terms you will have a very good idea how your child is progressing with reading because you are sharing books and listening to him read at home. There are, however, some general questions you might like to ask yourself about your son's or daughter's reading.

1 Does he still enjoy being read to?
2 Does he read to himself willingly and happily?
3 Is he able to discuss what he has been reading and show that he understands it?
4 Does he read a variety of things? For example:

humorous stories	jokes	detective stories
animal stories	poetry	historical fiction
adventure stories	magazines	science fiction
information books	comics	contemporary stories
classics	fantasy	

5 Does he belong to the public library?
6 Does he use books to find out things?
7 Is he able to choose information books appropriately, according to what he wants to find out?
8 Does he understand how to look things up in a contents page and an index?
9 Is he able to find out about something from a book and then tell you or write about it in his *own* words?
10 Does he read reasonably quickly?
11 Does he prefer reading silently to reading aloud?
12 When he's reading to you and he comes to a word he doesn't know does he:
   i) miss it out and read on (or re-read) and then guess?
   ii) continue only if what he says makes sense and sounds/looks right to him?
13 Does he read with reasonable accuracy? (eg does not constantly change tense or miss off endings)
14 Does he enjoy browsing around the library or bookshops with you?
15 Would he describe reading as one of the things he likes doing best?

The more times you can answer 'yes' the better your child is getting on with reading. 'No' answers indicate things you could encourage and support.

BOOKS FOR READERS ON THE MOVE: AGES 7+

Children of seven to nine years will be consolidating their early reading skills, developing fluency, confidence and stamina. The first two lists which follow are specifically for this age range in interest level: the first list containing shorter, simpler books – often light, amusing reads; the second list contains longer, more demanding books for children who are ready for a sustained read.

The list for children over nine years is intended as an initial guide to some of the best of children's fiction available today to buy or to borrow.

It is still important to read to your child, even when he is reading independently. Why? Because reading stories and poetry aloud is the best way to introduce children to new authors, to widen their reading diet and to persuade them to try them for themselves. The poetry, classics and folk tale lists contain books which are equally good to read aloud or for fluent readers to try for themselves.

First short novels etc: ages 7–9

The Appletree Man *Judith Stinton*
   Walker Read Alone 1989
A country story set in the last century about a girl who, with the help of the apple tree, defeats her greedy uncle.

Banana Books
   Heinemann
These are reasonably priced little hardback books written by top authors for newly independent readers. They cover a range of subjects from fantasy, animals, school stories. Below is a selection:

Beware, Princess!
Mary Hoffman
   1986
Poppy is an unconventional princess who deals with the traditional fairy story characters – ogres, knights and dragons – in an untraditional way.

The Erl King's Daughter
Joan Aiken
   1988
Kev's gran told him the story of the Erl King before she died but a nasty new girl at school frightens him by convincing him she is the Erl King's daughter.

Freckle Juice
Judy Blume
   1984
Andrew wants freckles, Nicky has freckles and doesn't want them and Sharon says she knows how to make freckles.

Storm
Kevin Crossley-Holland
   1985
A haunting story of wild, windswept marshes, a brave little girl and a mystery horseman.

The Bears On Hemlock Mountain *Alice Dalgliesh*
   Young Puffin 1989 (reissue)
When Jonathan has to go over the mountain to borrow his aunt's cooking pot, he keeps telling himself 'There ARE no bears on Hemlock Mountain' but he is not so sure.

Chips And Jessie *Shirley Hughes*
   Young Lion 1987
Shirley Hughes has made the step into more concentrated reading easier by breaking up her stories with comic strips and by having the characters speak directly to the reader. There are four stories about Chips and his friend, Jessie. For four more stories about Chips see: **Another Helping Of Chips**.

Count Boris Bolescu And The Black Pudding
Ann Jungman
   Young Corgi 1989
Count Boris is a geriatric vampire who cannot frighten young Mandy Bottomley from Lancashire, try as he might!

Dinner Ladies Don't Count *Bernard Ashley*
   Young Puffin 1984
Two school stories about two children with a problem, written with great insight.

Dragonfire *Ann Ruffell*
   Young Corgi 1987
Gribble the dragon has a problem – no fire. He is helped by Smith, a man who also has a problem. Four other titles.

Emily's Legs *Dick King-Smith*
   MacDonald 1988
Emily, the young spider, is rejected by the other spiders because she has ten legs.

E.S.P. *Dick King-Smith*
   Young Corgi 1989
The young pigeon's parents call him Eric Stanley Pigeon but the tramp in the park calls him E.S.P. for a different reason – he can peck winners from the racing pages!

Flat Stanley *Jeff Brown*
   Mammoth 1989
Stanley Lambchop wakes up one morning to discover that he has been flattened by his bedroom noticeboard. Being flat has its uses and Stanley has many adventures before regaining normal proportions. Also: **A Lamp For The Lambchops**.

Jets
   Young Lion
The format of this series is just right for young readers who want to read a 'proper' book but who have not developed the stamina required. They look like a paperback book, but chapters are short and the text is broken up by many different visual devices: eg cartoons, comic strips, speech bubbles, maps, diagrams etc. The attractive layout will entice children into reading. Some of the best so far are:

   Cowardy Cowardy Cutlass
   Robin Kingsland
      1989
   Peter the cabin-boy has to teach the feeble pirates how to be really fierce. Their test comes when Bloodthirsty Beryl attacks.

   Ging Gang Goolie, It's An Alien
   Bob Wilson
      1988
   The 3rd Balsawood Scout troop go to camp and meet Grott from the planet Grobblewockia.

Two Hoots
Helen Cresswell
   1988
The two Hoots are daft as coots so the other owls
threaten to turn them out of the wood, until Class
Four's nature trip.

The Little Dragon Steps Out *Ann Jungman*
   Young Corgi 1989
Janet gets a shock when the dragon steps out of her
book because he is going to be killed by a knight. He
refuses to go back until the story is changed.

Laura And The Bandits *Philippe Dumas*
   Young Lion 1982
On holiday with her family, Laura the sheepdog
discovers a cave full of stolen art treasures and helps
the police capture the bandits. Also: **Laura, Alice's
New Puppy**.

The Magic Finger *Roald Dahl*
   Young Puffin 1974
The girl who tells the story puts the magic finger on her
neighbours because they hunt wild animals. A very
moral and funny story.

The Nearly Terrible Birthday *Delia Huddy*
   Walker Read Alone 1989
Minty thinks everyone has forgotten her birthday
because her mother is in hospital.

The Shrinking Of Treehorn *Florence Parry Heide*
   Young Puffin 1975
Treehorn discovers that he is shrinking and no one
seems to care. Also: **Treehorn's Treasure**.

The Stolen Harvest; Romany Rat *Roger Williamson*
   Walker Read Alone 1989
Two books about Mary and Hubert, the cheesemaker
mice. Also recommended in the Walker Read Alone
series are: **Grandmother's Donkey** by Joan Smith;
Boo To A Goose by Judith Stinton.

The Story Of Ferdinand *Munro Leaf*
   Young Puffin 1977
As fresh now as when it was first written in 1937, this
little story tells of Ferdinand, the Spanish bull who
does not want to fight. Short and fairly simple.

T. R.'s Festival *Terrance Dicks*
   Young Corgi 1989
How the 'Fat Man', a teddy bear thief, is outwitted by
T. R. Bear, an American teddy bear who talks to his
owner, Jimmy. Four previous titles.

Wildcat Wendy *Nancy Chambers*
   Fontana Lion 1981
Wildcat Wendy and her trusty horse, Victor, deliver a
message to the Peekaboo Kid and fight off Headlock
Henry who is after the treasure. A female gallantly
holds her own in cowboy country.

Books for children of 7–9 years with more stamina

The Amazing Adventures Of Chilly Billy *Peter
Mayle*
   Magnet 1981
Find out what goes on in your fridge when the door is
shut.

A Bit Of Give And Take *Bernard Ashley*
   Young Corgi 1986
Scott finds a kitten trapped in the refuse bin to the flats
but the Council rule is 'No Pets'.

Clancy's Cabin *Margaret Mahy*
   Young Puffin 1987
Three children go on a camping holiday and discover
an old treasure map.

Clever Polly And The Stupid Wolf *Catherine Storr*
   Puffin 1967
Polly outwits the wolf who never gives up trying to eat
her. Also: **Polly And The Wolf Again**.

The Demon Bike Rider *Robert Leeson*
   Young Lion 1977
Mike and his friends think that the ghost seen on
Barker's Bonk is a joke, but is it?

Dog Powder *Mary Hoffman*
   Heinemann 1989
A boy's longing for a dog of his own, a pet shop with no
pets and a magic powder lead to the appearance and
disappearance of a variety of dogs.

Follow That Bus *Pat Hutchins*
 Young Lion 1979
Class Six get caught up in a bank robbery while on their farm outing. Also: **The House That Sailed Away; The Mona Lisa Mystery** and **The Curse Of The Egyptian Mummy**.

Flying Backwards *Barbara Giles*
 Puffin 1985
Magic bicycle oil sends Jack and Pug back in time.

George Speaks *Dick King-Smith*
 Kestrel Kites 1988 Hardback
George can talk like an adult and he is only four weeks old!

My Best Fiend *Sheila Lavelle*
 Fontana Lion 1980
There is never a dull moment being friends with Angela who is no angel. Also: **Trouble With The Fiend** and **The Fiend Next Door**.

My Naughty Little Sister And Bad Harry *Dorothy Edwards*
 Mammoth 1990
These simply-told stories of two naughty children are still very popular today. A cosy, relaxing read.

Rosie And The Boredom Eater *Helen Cresswell*
 Heinemann 1989
Rosie finds something in the dustbin which makes her day anything but boring.

Simon And The Witch *Margaret Stuart Barry*
 Lion 1976
Life is never dull for Simon whose best friend, the witch, can make all sorts of things happen. Also: **Return Of The Witch**.

Stig Of The Dump *Clive King*
 Puffin 1963
Barney falls into the disused chalk pit and finds a cave boy living there.

Tales Of A Fourth Grade Nothing *Judy Blume*
 Piper 1988
Peter finds life with a two-year-old brother very trying especially where his precious pet turtle, Dribble, is concerned. Also: **Superfudge**. (Note: Not all Judy Blume titles are suitable for this age range.)

Truant From Space *Brian Ball*
 Young Corgi 1988
Sam is truanting from his lessons back home on his distant planet. He joins Miss Denny's class and they help him escape from the truant-catchers, the Snoopy-Droops.

Ramona The Pest *Beverly Cleary*
 Puffin 1976
Wryly funny doings of an American kindergarten tot. (8–9 yrs.) Many more titles.

A Taste Of Blackberries *Doris Buchanan Smith*
 Puffin 1987
Coming to terms with the death of a friend and feelings of guilt.

Books for readers aged 9+

Asterix The Gaul *Goscinny & Uderzo*
 Hodder & Stoughton 1974
Comic-strip adventures of a band of Gauls resisting the Romans. Many other titles.

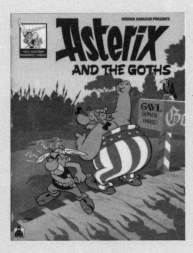

The Boy And The Whale *Katherine Scholes*
  Puffin 1985
One boy's struggle to save a beached whale.

Bumper Joke Book
  Collins 1989
Three joke books in one.

The Creature In The Dark *Robert Westall*
  Corgi 1989
Powerful story about a mystery sheep-killer.

Dangleboots *Dennis Hamley*
  Young Lion 1989
Football and adventure.

A Dog Called Nelson *Bill Naughton*
  Puffin 1984
Memories of a Lancashire boyhood.

The Fox Busters *Dick King-Smith*
  Puffin 1980
Hens versus foxes. Very funny.

The Ghost Of Thomas Kempe *Penelope Lively*
  Puffin 1984
A funny and historically interesting ghost story.

Goodnight Mister Tom *Michelle Magorian*
  Puffin 1983
Abused Willie is evacuated to the country and old Tom.
He blossoms as trust grows gradually. A deservedly
highly-acclaimed book.

The Great Puffin Joke Directory *Brough Girling*
  Puffin 1990
An A–Z of jokes. If you want a 'Doctor, doctor' joke,
just look under D!

Harriet The Spy *Louise Fitzhugh*
  Lion 1974
Harriet makes notes on all the goings-on in her
neighbourhood.

The Intergalactic Omniglot *Jenni Fleetwood*
  Corgi Yearling 1989
Science fiction.

Keeping Henry *Nina Bawden*
  Puffin 1989
A true story about an evacuee family rearing a baby
red squirrel.

A Little Lower Than The Angels *Geraldine
McCaughrean*
  Puffin 1989
Historical novel.

The Magic Camera *Adèle Geras*
  Young Corgi 1990
With the magic camera, Kaye finds out about her dead
mother whom she never knew.

The Midnight Fox *Betsy Byars*
  Puffin 1976
A boy and a fox.

Minnow On The Say *Philippa Pearce*
  Puffin 1978
Two boys, a canoe and a hunt for long-lost treasure.

The Silver Sword *Ian Serraillier*
  Puffin 1960
Adventure and survival in war-torn Poland.

Simon's Challenge *Theresa Breslin*
  Canongate Kelpie 1989
Detective story. Simon witnesses a computer theft.

The Turbulent Term Of Tyke Tiler *Gene Kemp*
  Puffin 1979
Trouble for Tyke at school.

Tom's Midnight Garden *Philippa Pearce*
  Puffin 1970
When the clock strikes thirteen, Tom goes back in time.

Up The Pier *Helen Cresswell*
  Puffin 1977
Clarrie meets an invisible family from the past.

Usborne Puzzle Adventures
  Usborne 1987/8
A story and brain teasers to solve as well: eg Time Train
To Ancient Rome; Danger At Demon's Cove.

The Warlock Of Firetop Mountain *Steve Jackson &
Ian Livingstone*
  Puffin 1982
Throw a dice, use skill and stamina and read your way
to your own adventure. 38 in this series of fighting
fantasy game books.

Woof! *Allan Ahlberg*
  Puffin 1987
The adventures of a boy who turns into a dog.

Classics

Alice's Adventures In Wonderland *Lewis Carroll*
  Julia MacRae 1988 Hardback
A new interpretation of this fantasy by
Anthony Browne.

Black Beauty *Anna Sewell*
  Picturemac 1989
A carefully adapted picture book version, lavishly
illustrated by Susan Jeffers.

premier
PICTUREMAC
Anna Sewell
BLACK BEAUTY
Adapted by ROBIN McKINLEY   *Pictures by* SUSAN JEFFERS

A Christmas Carol *Charles Dickens*
  Gollancz 1989
The tale of Tiny Tim and Scrooge, illustrated by
Michael Foreman.

Heidi *Johanna Spyri*
  Armada Classic 1989
A mountain childhood with grandfather.

Just So Stories *Rudyard Kipling*
  Picturemac 1985
In this series, each story is produced in a separate book,
beautifully illustrated by top children's illustrators
such as Michael Foreman, Charles Keeping and
Quentin Blake.

Peter Pan And Wendy *J. M. Barrie*
  Hodder and Stoughton 1976 Hardback
A pocket-sized book with black-and-white line drawings
by Shirley Hughes.

The Railway Children *E. Nesbit*
   Puffin Classic 1960
The children don't know where father is or when he will return.

The Secret Garden *Frances Hodgson Burnett*
   Puffin Classic 1951
Lonely orphaned Mary goes to live with her uncle and discovers a magical secret garden behind a locked door.

What Katy Did *Susan Coolidge*
   Armada Classics 1987
Tomboy Katy has a terrible accident and learns to be patient.

The Wind In The Willows *Kenneth Grahame*
   Puffin 1983
New pictures by John Burningham of the exploits of Toad and friends.

Myths, legends, folk and fairy tales

Alan Garner's Book Of British Fairy Tales
   Collins 1988
Powerful retellings of traditional tales. With an eye-catching title page for each story by Derek Collard.

The Amazing Adventures Of . . . Hercules; Jason; Ulysses
   Usborne 1982
Full-colour comic strip versions of these legendary heroes, simply retold. (7–9 years.)

A Book Of Enchantments And Curses
Ruth Manning-Saunders
   Magnet 1978
Lively, utterly readable versions of fairy tales from around the world. Many other titles, all well worth reading: eg **A Book Of Dragons; A Book Of Magic Animals**.

The Enchanted World: Parts One & Two
Amabel Williams-Ellis
   Picturemac 1988
Stories from around the world retold by an expert in the art of storytelling and wonderfully illustrated by Moira Kemp.

Sir Gawain And The Loathly Lady *Retold by Selina Hastings*
   Walker 1987
A beautiful version of this legend of knightly chivalry. The intricate medieval looking pictures and decorative borders by Juan Wijngaard make this a book to treasure.

Robin Hood And The Miller's Son; Robin Hood And Little John *Julian Atterton*
   Walker Story Book 1989
Two exciting adventures of Robin Hood and his merry men.

Seasons Of Splendour *Madhur Jaffrey*
   Puffin 1987
These Indian tales, myths, legends and explanations of the various religious festivals follow the Hindu calendar through the year. Stunning illustrations by Michael Foreman. For fluent readers of 9 + or to read aloud.

Tales Of The Greek Heroes *Roger Lancelyn Green*
   Puffin 1958
Masterly retellings, each tale connected to the one before. (10 + .)

The Wild Swans *Hans Christian Andersen (retold by Amy Ehrlich)*
   Picturemac 1989
Elise's love and loyalty eventually triumphs and she changes her brothers back into princes. This picture book edition is exquisitely illustrated by Susan Jeffers.

Poetry for readers aged 7+

Hiawatha's Childhood *Henry Wadsworth Longfellow*
   Picture Puffin 1986
Errol Le Cain's dark, atmospheric illustrations perfectly complement this extract from Longfellow's epic poem.

Jabberwocky *Lewis Carroll*
   Hodder & Stoughton 1988
A brilliantly coloured and intricately illustrated
version of this nonsense poem from *Alice Through the
Looking Glass*.

Jack The Treacle Eater *Charles Causley*
   Picturemac 1989
Haunting line drawings by Charles Keeping accompany
these poems and ballads steeped in legend.

Nailing The Shadow *Roger McGough*
   Puffin 1989
For older children to read alone – they will appreciate
the visual impact and verbal play of this collection of
McGough's poetry.

Please Mrs Butler *Allan Ahlberg*
   Puffin 1984
A collection of witty poems about primary school.

A Pot Of Gold *Unearthed by Jill Bennett*
   Doubleday Hardback 1989
This 'treasure-trove' of poems contains some real
nuggets and gems both old and new . . .

Quick, Let's Get Out Of Here *Michael Rosen*
   Puffin 1984
Michael Rosen's poems speak directly to children, in
their language.

Revolting Rhymes *Roald Dahl*
   Picture Puffin 1984
Typical Dahl versions of six well-known nursery tales
which are wickedly funny. Read aloud or for fluent
readers to read alone. Also: **Dirty Beasts**.

Books to read
to children aged 7 +

Bedknob And Broomstick *Mary Norton*
   Puffin 1970
Three children fly back and forth in time at the twist of
a knob on the old bed.

The BFG *Roald Dahl*
   Puffin 1984
We cannot forget Roald Dahl – the children won't let
us! All his books make marvellous read-alouds. This is
one of his best for the younger end of this age range.
The BFG (Big Friendly Giant) captures a little girl
called Sophie. Also: **Charlie And The Chocolate
Factory; James And The Giant Peach; The
Witches** and **Mathilda**. For older children, **Danny,
The Champion Of The World**. Fluent readers will
enjoy reading them all for themselves.

Bonny's Big Day *James Herriot*
   Picture Piper 1989
James Herriot persuades Mr Skipton to enter Bonny,
the old cart horse, into the Family Pets' Class at the
Darroby Show – with surprising results. One of the
great charms of this book are the pictures by Ruth
Brown.

Daggy Dogfoot *Dick King-Smith*
   Puffin 1982
The adventures of a brave little pig who can swim.

The Kingdom Under The Sea *Joan Aiken*
   Puffin 1973
Haunting stories from Eastern Europe told by a
wonderful storyteller with fascinating silhouettes by
Jan Pienkowski.

The Lion, The Witch And The Wardrobe *C. S. Lewis*
   Lion 1980
Peter, Susan, Edmond and Lucy go through the
wardrobe into the Land of Narnia where danger and
excitement lie. Many children will want to hear or read
all the Narnia books after this one.

Little House In The Big Woods *Laura Ingalls Wilder*
   Puffin 1963
The first in a series about the life of a pioneering
American family told by the author about her childhood.

Stories For Nine-Year-Olds *Edited by Sara & Stephen
Corrin*
   Puffin 1981
A good thick collection of traditional tales, myths,
legends and stories.

CHILDREN WITH SPECIAL NEEDS

Reading problems

Difficulties with reading affect both boys and girls, men and women. But it is the case that there are more males with reading problems than there are females. We often tend to lump reading difficulties together as one problem but, of course, given any group of half a dozen adults or children, the nature and reasons for the problems could all be different. Let's look at a few examples to illustrate this. They are fictional examples but they *do* represent what can happen in real life.

MARTIN is eight. He was very late in learning to talk and only stopped having speech therapy last year. He is quite good at working out how to pronounce words and can just about cope with books which most seven-year-olds manage well. The main trouble is that he reads in a monotone and doesn't really appear to understand too much of what he is reading.

BECKY is nine. She has learning difficulties which make most school work very hard for her. Her parents describe Becky as not very bright but a very helpful and loving daughter. She is popular with children and teachers at school, which she enjoys even though the work is very hard for her.

DARREN is ten and a great footballer. Generally very sports-minded, he is an extremely active boy who is on the go all the time. He likes maths and science but hates reading and writing. His mum says it is a real effort to get him to read at home and when he does it often ends up with frayed tempers. He says he's going to be a professional footballer so it doesn't matter if he cannot read very well – and 'stories are stupid, anyway.'

MARIK is ten and got off to a slow start in reading at school because he had a great deal of time off through ill health. He was about three years behind with his reading when he was eight, so his parents paid for private lessons for him. This teacher gave him a lot of work in phonics and building up words and then the lessons had to stop because Marik's parents could not afford them any longer. He is now reading at the level of the average eight-year-old but doesn't seem to be making any further progress.

ROSA-LEE is eight. Her reading had been coming along very well but in the last year she seems to have slipped back. In the last 12 months Rosa-Lee's parents have been through a very bitter divorce. At a recent parents' evening her teacher told Rosa-Lee's father (who has custody) that his daughter seems to have lost interest in reading and school work generally.

CARLA is nine and her parents had noticed several things over the last few years: she had great problems in learning her left and right, in learning the days of the week and in following instructions. She loved listening to stories when she was little and still enjoys being read to now. Her level of reading is very poor and her writing consists largely of bizarre spellings. Her younger sister, however, reads and writes extremely well. Carla appears to be just as bright as her sister and she does do well in oral work at school. She has recently seen an educational psychologist because both the school and her parents are worried by her lack of progress. The educational psychologist has advised that Carla is dyslexic.

Each one of the above fictional children has some kind of problem with reading and each one obviously needs help. What could we say about their learning needs and how their parents might help?

MARTIN

Children who have language difficulties in their early years miss out on a lot of other learning too. In learning to talk, children also learn not only about the world of ideas but also how language works. What can parents of children like Martin do to help their reading?

- Firstly they must remember that he has been delayed in reading because of the slow start in talking, so he needs extra input: they should read lots of stories and books to him, talk about and discuss what has been read, checking that he understands both the words and the ideas.
- It is very important that Martin reads books which are not too difficult for him. He needs lots of 'easy' reading to consolidate what he is learning and get to grips with meaning and the idea that a text has to make sense. If a book is challenging in terms of the number of unfamiliar words, he won't be able to do this.

Using a tape recorder can provide a child with necessary feedback about his reading.

- He should, even more than most children, be encouraged to guess unfamiliar words by asking what would make sense there and to check his guesses to make sure that they do.
- His parents should make sure that at the end of his reading session they discuss in detail what he has read: 'Tell me about what we've been reading . . . Why did —— happen? . . . What do you think —— means?' and so on.
- Children who read with little or no expression need to be encouraged to make their reading sound more like talking. It is, however, almost impossible for children to monitor or even realise how they sound while they are actually reading. Using a tape recorder to read passages into can be a great help; children can practise by themselves, trying to put more expression into their reading and getting immediate feedback from the tape as to how they sound.

It is worth pointing out that one of the most general causes of children reading without expression or in a monotone is that they are reading material which is too difficult for them – all their energy and concentration goes on actually decoding the words, and meaning and expression naturally suffer. This is true for all children.

BECKY

People are different – we look different and we have different strengths and weaknesses. Some of us find working with our hands very hard and some of us find working with our brains equally hard. Becky and children like her will never be intellectual giants but that is no reason why they cannot learn to read. It will simply take longer. The world's great works of literature may always be beyond Becky, but given time and patience she will achieve a standard of reading that could enable her to hold down a job, deal with the everyday world and, if she wishes, use reading for recreation too. Children like Becky need:

- Lots of listening to stories and books read by parents. Not only does this help to keep alive the pleasure of books for the child who finds reading difficult, but it also offers lots to talk and think about, thus providing stimulation as well as pleasure. Becky, for example, might enjoy fairy and folk tales or stories about animals.
- It takes slower-learning children longer to build up a vocabulary of words which are remembered and recognised

on sight. This can be helped in various ways.

For example, by:

- using books to share and read aloud which have lots of natural repetition and repeating phrases in them
- tackling the reading of high frequency words (when, so, because etc) through spelling using the *Look, Cover, Write, Check* method outlined on pages 119–120.
- playing reading games. The game described on page 79 which deals with teaching letter sounds can be used with whole words written on cards so that the idea is to match a pair of words (here, here; then, then etc.).

Bingo is fun and most children enjoy playing it. The game can be made using words instead of numbers.

To make:

Make a different baseboard for each player (including you) as shown below. Choose a basic 17 or so words: eg

when	this	here	the	and	because
which	what	there	so	they	if
that	children	for	with	will	then

As well as writing a selection of the words on each board, write each of the words on a separate square of card.

To play:

Shuffle the pack of word cards and turn them face down. Pick up the first card, show it to the other players and say what it is. Players look to see if the word is on their baseboard. If it is, they cover that square with a counter or slip of paper. The first player to cover their board is the winner.

After a few games, get your child to try to read each word as it is turned up.

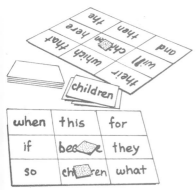

Bingo is an entertaining way of learning words.

DARREN

Some children are very good at persuading themselves that reading is unimportant if they find it difficult. They do so (unconsciously) to protect their self-esteem. Children do, however, need to be motivated to read if they are to make progress. As a parent you have to try and persuade a child that reading *is* important through reasons that the individual *child* appreciates. 'To get on in school' or 'to get a good job' are reasons which are too vague, too remote or inappropriate for children like Darren. He needs to be persuaded within the context of his own (realistic or otherwise) ambitions because *that* is what is important to him. Professional footballers need reading and writing for a range of reasons – not least because they cannot play football all their lives! Darren's parents could make a list with him of all the things for which reading and writing would be necessary.

For example:
- replying to fan letters (!)
- reading to pass the time on long journeys to away matches
- reading match reports in the newspapers to see how the competition is doing
- writing a weekly column in a newspaper when he is famous.

The actual reading at home needs to be in short bursts and it is sensible to try stories with a link to the child's interest – in this case football – or to non-fiction – related or otherwise. Reluctant readers often accept non-fiction more readily. Usborne, for example, publish a huge range of plentifully illustrated information books. Don't forget newspapers or special interest magazines that you can read together.

Another idea for children like this is to get them to write their 'life-story' – in this case Darren, as a famous footballer writes about, for example, his lifestyle and famous matches. Alternatively, he could make, using a scrapbook, a football book concerning anything that catches his fancy on the subject – from rules, to famous teams, to match reports of his own games.

Most children have ambitions which they enjoy writing about.

MARIK

Many parents consider private lessons if their child has reading difficulties. If this is something you have thought about, it is crucial that the private teacher really knows about the teaching of reading and is both up-to-date and well-informed about what is needed. It is also important that the teacher is used to dealing with pupils of the particular age group and, crucially, that your child will get on with him or her.

Sometimes an emphasis on phonics teaching for a short while can help some children who may be 'stuck' in the early stages of reading. But it can then appear almost as if a plateau is reached. This is the case with Marik, our fictional example. What Marik and children like him need is:

- Encouragement to read widely at their current achievement level in order to consolidate and apply the skills that have been acquired in a fairly short time.
- Encouragement/teaching to use additional ways of tackling unfamiliar words. 'Sounding out' or 'building up' words does not always work and so it is vital that a child is helped to use context too. (See the section on listening to reading on pages 70–71.)
- The continuation of listening to books read aloud at home – to keep alive the pleasure in reading and to introduce more demanding reads and more sophisticated language use than the children can manage for themselves.

ROSA-LEE

Rosa-Lee is typical of children who have recently faced or are facing some kind of emotional trauma. This can be caused by many things; for example, the death of a parent or a close family member, bullying at school, divorce or the death of a beloved pet. As adults we know that if we are facing something stressful or painful in our lives, we find it hard to concentrate on other things. Children are no different. When they are faced with a problem (be it major or minor in our eyes) they find it hard to concentrate on school work and may well 'slip back'.

Children who are experiencing some emotional crisis or problem need support and understanding. Often we cannot solve the serious problems but we can help them to adjust to changed circumstances. Rosa-Lee and children like her can be helped by:

- Encouraging them to talk about the problem and being a sympathetic but realistic listener. Some children find it difficult to talk initially. Often, a book can be the first step in facing up to something like death or divorce and you will find a few suggestions on page 137. Hearing or reading about someone else with a similar problem helps the child to appreciate that he or she is not unique in this respect.
- Trying to make sure that the child does not feel guilty for what has happened. It is by no means unusual to hear of children who believe that it is because of something they have done or not done, or because of the kind of person they are that their parents have split up. Such instances need constant and determined efforts at reassurance on the parents' part.
- Remembering that it is quite normal and usual for some ground to be lost at school under such circumstances. Give the child time to come to terms with what has happened and don't worry – lost ground can be made up later.
- Acknowledging that major changes in family circumstances affect everyone involved and parents have to deal with their own grief, anger, loss and so on. Despite the need to cope at their own level, parents should try to make time to support their bewildered, anxious or upset children and try to ensure that everyday routines are maintained as far as possible. One such routine may be the reading and sharing of a book at bedtime. It is an important opportunity for closeness, talk and reassurance. The magic of a book can make bedtime thoughts happy ones.

CARLA

For some parents it is a relief to find out that their child is dyslexic; for others it brings fresh anxiety. Let's look at a few of the issues involved.

Dyslexia is also known as 'specific learning difficulty' (often the preferred term). It refers to children who have serious difficulty with written symbols despite having received good schooling, being of normal intelligence and so on. Two children sitting side by side could have very different 'symptoms' of their difficulty. For example: one could be described as clumsy, the other not; one could carry two or three linked instructions in his head, the other not; one could have a good visual memory, the other not. Yet both could be dyslexic. As far as we can tell, there are a range of possible features which characterise dyslexics but any one individual is highly unlikely to have them all. To be dyslexic is to have several of the associated features and not just one. Lots of children, for example, have difficulty in remembering the sequence of days of the week or months of the year. This in itself does not necessarily mean that they are dyslexic.

As you will have gathered by now, dyslexia is *not* something for the average class teacher or parent to diagnose – it takes specialist knowledge. A child who is suspected of being dyslexic needs to be assessed by an educational psychologist. Educational psychologists are *not* to be confused with psychiatrists! They are simply specialists in children's learning (unlike psychiatrists, who deal with mental illness).

A child who is diagnosed as dyslexic needs specialist teaching which is carefully structured. The specialist teacher can also give individual parents specific advice on how best to support their child. In general terms, however, dyslexic children benefit from parental support in some of the ways already outlined. For example, from:
- listening to and sharing books
- learning words for both reading and spelling through the technique outlined on pages 119–120
- playing reading games (for learning both letter sounds and whole words) which offer lots of practice in an enjoyable and not boring way: eg Bingo (see page 111).

It is likely that the specialist teaching will involve a lot of sounds and letter pattern work. It is most important, therefore, that dyslexic children continue to have access to books at home which are fun, enjoyable and can be shared with a parent time and time again.

If you suspect your child may be dyslexic you should ask the school, as is your right, for your child to be seen by an educational psychologist. If you happen to live in a part of the country where there is a branch of the Dyslexia Institute you can pay for a private assessment. The Dyslexia Institute also offers specialist tuition – as do most local education authorities (see page 140 for their address).

Almost without exception, children who have any kind of reading difficulty benefit from what is known as Paired Reading. This technique has been widely used by schools and parents working together and there have often been dramatic improvements made in children's reading. Usually it is undertaken for about an eight-week period at a time and involves parent and child for ten minutes a day. The books or other reading material are chosen *by the child* and the following procedure is used:

First step: Reading together

- You and your child read out loud together.
- To help you keep together, your child points to the words as you both read and you adjust your reading speed to the pointing.
- When your child hesitates or makes a mistake, you wait no longer than five seconds before saying the word.
- Your child repeats the word and the reading continues.

Paired Reading is a technique which has produced impressive results with children who find reading difficult.

Second step: Reading alone

- When your child feels confident enough and wishes to read alone, he signals to you to stop reading. This is a prearranged signal and can be whatever suits you both – a nudge or a tap on the book, for example.
- When your child hesitates or makes a mistake, you wait no longer than five seconds before supplying the word.
- Your child repeats the word.
- You and your child continue reading aloud together as in the first step until your child signals to you again to stop reading.

You will find that it takes two or three sessions at least to get used to the procedure, which does need to be followed as explained in order for it to be most effective. Keeping the reading aloud in step or synchronised is probably the most difficult aspect, but it is made easier by your child pointing so that you are reading at a speed which suits him. If your child has any kind of reading difficulty, do try Paired Reading. Lots of research projects have been carried out to judge how effective it is and the results are generally impressive.

Quite naturally, parents *do* worry if their child has a problem with reading, but there are several ways in which you can support and help:

- Try not to let your anxiety become obvious to your child. If you have to discuss the problem with the school, don't do it in front of your son or daughter.
- If your child has brothers or sisters who *can* read (especially if they are younger children) try to ensure that your reading sessions do not take place in front of them. It can be disheartening or embarrassing for a child with difficulties to read in front of brothers and sisters who read easily and well.
- Talk to your child about the reading difficulty and acknowledge that the problem exists. Explain that many people have trouble in learning to read; point out all the things that he *can* do; say how proud you are of his efforts to overcome his difficulties; assure him that he doesn't have to solve the problem alone and that you and the school will help.
- Look through this section again, and even if the fictional

children don't match your child, look at all the suggestions and see if there is something you haven't thought of doing which you could try.

- Do your utmost to praise and encourage all your child's attempts and achievements. Remember, children don't choose to have reading difficulties and they would dearly like to overcome them. You can help them to do just that.

SPELLING PROBLEMS

All children who have reading difficulties have some spelling difficulties too, but not all children who have spelling problems have reading difficulties – the two do not *always* go hand in hand.

In the past, many parents have been told that if their child with spelling difficulties can be encouraged to read more then the spelling will improve. This is simply not so. Spelling and reading are two opposite sides of the coin of written language. In reading, readers don't look at every single letter, but in writing we *must* know the letter-by-letter structure of words. Spelling and reading are different. All that reading may do is to improve knowledge and experience of words generally; it may extend children's vocabulary but it won't teach them how to spell those words.

Children with spelling problems have got to be taught to spell – how to learn words, how to use a dictionary and how to proof-read their writing to find mistakes. As with many other things, the older a person or child is, the harder it is to remedy matters. With the new National Curriculum, however, children with spelling difficulties should be identified and helped earlier because spelling is now an Attainment Target in its own right.

Spelling is largely to do with our *visual* memory for words and patterns rather than our auditory memory. In other words, for English spelling the important thing is how words look and not how they sound.

The most crucial aspect of helping children is to give them a technique for learning words that encourages the use of visual memory and, moreover, one that actually works. The most effective technique which is used in schools is known as the *Look, Cover, Write, Check* routine which has been promoted by the country's leading authorities on spelling, Margaret Peters and Charles Cripps.

It's our visual memory of words which tells us when a spelling looks wrong.

Look, Cover, Write, Check

In detail, this means teaching children to:

- LOOK at the word carefully in order to remember it. Look at any awkward bits (eg two *t*s in putting); make links with other words (there is a hen in w*hen* or a hat in w*hat*); perhaps say the word as it is spelled and not usually pronounced (eg Wed-nes-day or magic-Ian).
- SAY the word as you look at it
- COVER the word with a finger, piece of card or a bookmark
- WRITE the word from memory
- CHECK what you have written by looking at the word again. If what you did was not correct, which bit of the word caused the problem?
- REPEAT the steps until you can write the word quickly and easily from memory without really thinking about it.

This method is hard work. It is much easier for children to copy instead of writing a word from memory. BUT, endless copying of a word doesn't actually fix it or put it into spelling memory. So children need to be encouraged and reminded to use the technique all the time when they need to learn words. If children are taught the method from an early stage it *does* become a habit. Older children who are aware of their spelling difficulty but who have not learned the technique need to have it proved that it will work.

If this is the case for your child, then ask him or her for a word which they would like to be able to spell but cannot. Then say something like: 'OK, I'm going to show you how to learn the word and in five or ten minutes you *will* be able to spell it.' If your child volunteers a very long word then say that it might take a little longer and break the word into two or three parts. Treat each part as a separate 'word'; go through the steps for each and then go through the steps for the whole word: eg *budgerigar – budge* and *rigar* then *budgerigar*.

When your child asks you how to spell something at home, don't just spell out the letters for him: write the word down so that he can *see* what it looks like. It's quite a good idea to keep a little notebook handy just for this purpose. You can then choose words for your child to actually learn. Don't worry overmuch about words like *pterodactyl*, but do concentrate on the words that children use frequently in writing: eg because, when, were, afterwards, only, these, very, there, their, number words, question words etc.

If it is at all possible, try to make links with words your child may already know: eg can spell *here*, but not *where*. Group words according to their visual pattern, regardless of the way they are pronounced. For example:

her	*one*	*watch*	*read*	*our*
there	*done*	*matches*	*tread*	*your*
where	*gone*	*catch*	*bread*	*four*
here	*alone*	*patch*	*bead*	*flour*
mo*ther*	*shone*	*scratch*	*head*	*journey*
fa*ther*				*hour*

Give your child a group of words like these and see if he can put them into one sentence (the sillier the better!) and then write it. For example:

- M*ove* over l*ove*, you're sitting on the *oven*.
- He c*augh*t his n*augh*ty d*augh*ter l*augh*ing.
- W*atch* out, you'll c*atch* it if you play with m*atch*es.
- I *eat* p*each*es, ice-cream, br*ead* and p*eas* *each* t*ea*-time.
- I th*ough*t he *ough*t to run thr*ough* it alth*ough* he had a bad c*ough*.

Other hints

1 Don't let your child feel unique in not being able to spell. Assure him that lots of people have difficulty with spelling and say how proud you are of the effort to improve.
2 Do try to get your child to use a dictionary. This is not easy and you will need to provide a lot of help and support but it *is* worth persevering. Use a children's dictionary – not an adult one.
3 Get your child to try to identify his own spelling errors in a piece of writing by lightly underlining words which he thinks he may have spelled wrongly. Go over them with him and then choose four or five for him to learn in the way outlined.

PHYSICAL PROBLEMS

Most children who have severe physical difficulties or sensory impairments are identified early in life and receive specialist help. But many children have lesser problems which are harder to detect and which can easily be missed. All children who cannot hear or see clearly, or who find it hard to hold a book still, or who suffer from conditions such as migraine or diabetes may well experience difficulties in learning to read. Children who are receiving medication for conditions such as asthma may also have problems in this area. It is essential to understand the nature of these special needs. Parents and teachers should know what to look for and then what to do if a specific difficulty is suspected.

Hearing Loss

There is a common cry from parents and teachers: 'He can hear when he wants to!' All parents know that a favourite TV programme is more interesting to children than anything the parents may be saying to them at the time. However, it is estimated that at least 20 per cent of children suffer from a hearing loss at some time in their school career. This type of hearing loss is mild and varies – children hear clearly one week but miss much of what is being said the next. This is annoying for parents, who may feel their child is being deliberately difficult. It is far more annoying and frustrating for the child! This type of hearing loss is associated with heavy colds, ear infections, 'flu and catarrh. It makes the child, already feeling unwell, also feel left out and confused. Fluid which remains in the middle part of the ear causes a condition called 'glue ear'. This loss is called a *conductive loss* or *middle ear problem*. It can usually be treated medically by using antibiotics. Sometimes surgery is used to drain out fluid and a small tube, called a grommet, can be inserted into the eardrum to help keep the ear healthy. For a small number of children this kind of loss can become almost a permanent state of affairs. In such cases a small hearing aid may be fitted. Down's Syndrome children in particular are prone to such problems.

Every class at school contains children with a conductive hearing loss. Difficulties in developing clear speech, in understanding and in reading, may well be wrongly classed as due to laziness, lack of attention, or poor general ability. A hearing loss can make spoken language muffled, misheard, incomplete or misunderstood. The effects may be considerable.

All children should have their hearing tested during the pre-school years and on entry to school or shortly afterwards. If your child has missed these tests ask your doctor or Health Visitor to arrange for one to be carried out. It is possible for children who have passed these tests to be found to have a hearing loss at a later date. This may be because the testing wasn't carefully controlled. For example, the child may have responded to a slight movement or a shadow rather than turning on hearing the sound. All appears well until the child's speech develops slowly or speech sounds are very poor. Further tests of hearing must then be carried out. It is also possible that, on first testing, the hearing was normal but the hearing loss has been acquired later. This can follow an illness or an accident.

Meningitis, measles, mumps, chicken-pox, viral pneumonia, 'flu, kidney infections and diabetes can all have a hearing loss as a side effect. Accidents involving the skull sometimes cause a hearing loss. In cases of injury or serious illness (such as meningitis) hearing tests should be carried out routinely but parents can insist on their child's hearing being tested *if they have any suspicions about it at all*. The degree of loss resulting from illness may vary from mild to profound. It is not only the loudness of sound that will be affected but also the quality. Sound may well be distorted. If hearing aids are prescribed the child will have the support from a qualified teacher of the hearing-impaired.

Recognising a hearing loss can be difficult. Children may respond to a clap of the hands, to a rustle of sweet papers or to a clanking of keys. This tells us a child has some hearing but nothing else. An accurate test gives two important pieces of information. It tells how loud a sound must be to be heard and what kind of sound can be heard – low, medium or high pitch. This information is needed for each ear. When the tester is confident that hearing alone, with no visual clues, has been tested then hearing levels can be established. Hearing loss can now be ruled out as a cause for concern or medical or remedial action can be taken if necessary. Parents cannot test hearing accurately but their observations give a lot of useful information to the tester.

Any child who has difficulty in developing spoken language should have their hearing tested. Children with only mild losses may miss out sounds from their speech. Vowel sounds are louder than consonants so rarely present a problem. Weaker consonants are more easily misheard or missed altogether. In this way 'fish' may be misheard and children may say 'tish' or 'ish'; 'ice-cream' may become 'i-kee'. Most young children use their own words for everyday objects and all young children substitute one sound for another. If, however, a child fails to develop more sounds or always has difficulty with particular sounds then seek the advice of your doctor or health visitor. It is probably part of the natural development of sounds but it could be a hearing problem.

When parents seek professional advice it is very helpful if they can pass on as much information as possible – so what should they look out for? What signs may point to a hearing loss?

- A child who appears to be day-dreaming or 'lost in their own little world' may be bored with trying to listen to mumbled indistinct speech and have retreated to find their interests elsewhere. The particularly quiet child may have lost the thread of the conversation because of an inability to hear all of what is said. To avoid looking 'silly' some children avoid situations which highlight the difficulties they face.

Is he being difficult or can he not hear?

- In contrast, a child who has particularly loud speech may be trying to dominate conversations. This allows the child to know what is being talked about and to be included more often. In noisy conditions it is natural to raise your voice. It is hard for a child with a hearing loss to know just how loud their voice sounds.

- A child who often asks strange questions and who frequently misunderstands or copies from the child next to him may be responding to hearing incomplete questions or to mishearing information. A simple comment such as 'Shall we go for a swim?' could be misheard as 'Shall we go to the swings?' When a child says 'yes', and then says, 'Can I take my bike?' parents may well be puzzled. Why does he want his bicycle at the swimming pool? Surprise, laughter or irritation make the child feel difficult, foolish and annoyed. Reassurances from parents may well help but may also underline the child's feelings of frustration. Any of us who tries to join in a conversation and finds we have the wrong end of the stick knows how embarrassing it can be. To avoid these mistakes children may constantly seek attention and reassurance.

- Frustration can result in outbursts of temper tantrums. Most children display this behaviour from time to time but note whether your child also has a bad cold or catarrh, fails to respond to your voice normally, hears better when he can see you or appears to be the 'odd-one-out' at playgroup or at school. None of these are unusual on their own, but put together they point to the possibility of a hearing difficulty.

In school, children may show particular difficulty in following instructions, developing good reading skills, coping with dictated work, and in written work. *Middle ear problems* are common in young children – and the difficulties which arise from hearing loss can be put right and children given confidence to succeed.

It cannot be overstressed that all those concerned with children, parents, carers, teachers and the medical professions, should realise the importance of recognising a mild hearing loss. The first line of action is to consult your doctor or health visitor. If you feel that insufficient importance is being attached to your child's loss, ask to be referred to an ear, nose and throat specialist. In extreme cases, where parents suspect a hearing loss and are having difficulties in obtaining advice or getting a hearing test, they should contact the

National Deaf Children's Society who will advise on local facilities and contacts (see page 140 for the address).

Visual impairment

Vision and visual skills are an extremely important part of any child's development. It is estimated that 80 per cent of school tasks rely on a child's ability to use his vision effectively. Serious and severe visual difficulties are usually diagnosed early in life as a result of medical checks and routine screening procedures. As with hearing impairments, severe or profound difficulties are most readily diagnosed. Mild or acquired difficulties are more easily missed. Even mild visual impairments if unnoticed can have considerable effects on a child.

Types and causes of visual impairment

SQUINT

One of the most obvious visual problems recognised by parents is a squint. This is when the eyes fail to work together, and the eyes can be seen to be looking in different directions. There are several types of squint and several different causes for the condition. The important point here is that we use two eyes working together to give us depth perception. This enables us to see in three dimensions, to see the shape and position of objects. In the case of a squint, the vision in one eye is suppressed, allowing the other eye to focus and avoiding 'double-vision'. Medical advice should be sought from your doctor or health visitor who will ensure both eyes are encouraged to work. The sooner help is made available the better. Failure to correct a squint can lead to loss of central vision in the poorer eye and an inability to develop 'binocular-vision'. This is helpful in judging distances, coping with steps, outdoor games and many more everyday situations.

Several common eye defects are related to the failure of the eyes to focus rays of light on the retina at the back of the eye.

SHORT SIGHT OR MYOPIA

This occurs when the eyeball is slightly too long. Light rays which should focus at the back of the eye focus in front of the retina. This makes objects which are at a distance appear blurred although close-up objects are seen normally.

LONG SIGHT OR HYPERMETROPIA

This occurs when the eyeball is too short. The light rays focus behind the retina. Objects in the distance appear normally but those which are close appear blurred.

ASTIGMATISM

An astigmatism occurs when the cornea, which is at the front of the eye and is usually evenly curved, is not smoothly rounded. This distorts the light rays and the eye sees a distorted picture. There are several types of astigmatism and most can be corrected.

Vision is a learned skill. Children learn to co-ordinate their eyes by experience. They learn to use their eyes together to look at an object. They learn to adjust the eye to see objects at close range and again at a distance. Eyes help us to make sense of the world, to manipulate objects within it and to move freely. If everything is seen as blurred or fuzzy round the edges, or there appear to be two objects instead of only one then the brain tells the child this is normal. The brain compensates for this and the child learns to cope with the surroundings. Only careful observation and testing help to establish a child's particular area of difficulty so that appropriate action can be taken. Parents who suspect visual difficulties but find it hard to get access to the system should contact the Royal National Institute For The Blind (RNIB) who can advise on all aspects of visual impairment (see page 140 for their address).

Finally, children may acquire a visual impairment as the result of illness or injury. Parents should immediately report any apparent difficulties they notice to their doctor or health visitor.

As with hearing impairment there are a number of signs which should be noted and passed on to your doctor or health visitor. Some children complain of gritty or dusty eyes. Young children, who are unable to tell you that their eyes are uncomfortable, are likely to let you know in other ways. Children will rub their eyes repeatedly, screw them up in bright light or may blink their eyes repeatedly. Other signs of

*Is she timid? Immature?
Or does it all look a blur
to her?*

eye problems are swollen lids, eyes which look inflamed or
cloudy, or wobbly eyes which move on their own. Parents are
usually quick to spot these difficulties and equally quick to
take action.

What other indicators should parents watch out for? Which
are less immediately obvious but equally important?

- A child who has poor balance and finds difficulty going down
  steps or who frequently bumps into objects at the side or
  near his feet may not merely be timid. General clumsiness
  may be the result of poor co-ordination or lack of
  concentration. It may result from a mild physical difficulty
  or the inability to see objects clearly.
- A child who pulls 'odd' faces or who turns his head to one
  side or even closes one eye may well be struggling to bring
  an object into focus.
- Children may choose to play with toys very close up or at
  arm's length in order to try to compensate for a visual
  problem. Similarly, sitting in a very twisted or awkward
  position when working may be simply another method of
  overcoming a distorted visual pattern.
- Playgroups and playgrounds can present quite threatening
  situations to children with vision problems, where a mass

of exciting toys or a busy playground is only seen as blurred and fragmented. It is often easier to simply withdraw than to attempt to make sense of the blur and join in.

- If a child suddenly starts to complain of headaches or dizziness it is always wise to think carefully about the situation and consider medical advice. It is too easy to discount a genuine difficulty simply because a child finds it hard to explain exactly how he feels.
- Children who have difficulty in matching colours, producing sequences of colours and in interpreting some pictures may simply be colour-blind. This is a condition which affects boys predominantly but not exclusively.

Colour-blindness is not blindness at all but an inability to see certain colours. Usually, the ability to see various shades of green and red is impaired. A holly tree covered in berries may appear to be all shades of one colour rather than red berries sharply contrasting to green leaves. There is no treatment for colour-blindness but knowledge of the condition may help parents to accept red grass and green houses from children who are of an age to have left these colour combinations behind them.

Children who suffer from migraine may, in addition to having severe headaches and a feeling of nausea, be disturbed by bright zigzag lines or flashes. Regular migraine attacks make it particularly difficult for a child to concentrate on reading.

Some children suffer from tinnitus, or noises produced inside the sufferer's head. These noises can be very loud and distressing and make concentrating on any task difficult. There are also many children who, despite the fact that they have 'normal' hearing and vision, are unable to make use of the information they receive. These children may attend for repeated hearing and vision tests before being discharged. They require skilled teaching and carefully structured programmes to allow them to make sense of the information being received by the brain.

Learning to read

Many skills which are developed in the pre-school years form the base upon which reading skills will rest. The development of listening skills – recognising different types of sound, different rhythms and stresses, the patterns contained within spoken language, an understanding of rhymes – depends on being able to hear clearly. Many children fail to develop their listening skills to the full because their hearing varies so much. Lack of success gives children little incentive to try in areas they find difficult.

In addition to understanding sounds and the way sounds go together, reading involves understanding the meaning of what has been read. A child whose language development has been affected by a hearing loss may find words in print that he does not understand. Many books aimed at early readers introduce 'made-up' words to add fun and interest. Whilst a child with a visual impairment may really enjoy these fun words, a hearing impaired child may easily miss the whole point. An example of this is the word 'bommyknocker' used in the story of *The Hungry Giant* in the Storychest series published by E. J. Arnold. The majority of children love the sound of the word but a child with a hearing loss may have nothing to relate to it. Fortunately, the very visual nature of this story is likely to interest hearing impaired children too.

Reading schemes or reading games based on phonics – using the 'sounds' of letters to build up words – present obvious difficulties for hearing impaired children. Many people incorrectly assume that what is missed by the ears will be seen by the eye. But lipreading is not as simple as that! Words all sound different when spoken but many look identical to a lipreader. Some sounds are impossible to lipread. Lipreading is a skill demanding good light, a clear lip pattern, a good knowledge of language and a clear view of the speaker's face – even then it is problematic. It is not a relaxing or easy method of understanding speech.

At storytime, when giving instructions or explaining things, during discussions or when sharing a book, a hearing impaired child is at a disadvantage. Parents and teachers who take time to explain, who give extra clues, who help a child to join in are a child's best friend. Books which do not rely heavily on phonic skills – 'the cat on the mat' – but which are visually interesting, make good use of colour and of relevant pictures have much to offer. The English language adds its own problems for children with language difficulties. Words often sound identical but are written differently and have different meanings; for example, to, two, and too. In addition there are

words which look identical but which are pronounced differently according to the context: for example, tear – 'He shed a *tear* because she had a *tear* in her skirt.' Children who have a long-standing mild hearing loss may also fall into the trap of taking everything they read literally. Some examples of real mistakes are illustrated. Talking about what you or your child has read is the best way of identifying and overcoming such difficulties.

There are a host of visually interesting books; lift-the-flap, putting fingers through, with wheels attached or characters which can be moved from page to page. These books encourage active participation rather than relying only on the text to involve a child. An understanding of language and words develops more fully in a relaxed situation, as a child begins to understand that books are fun, reading will follow.

For children with an unrecognised visual problem or a known, severe visual difficulty, the printed word can obviously present problems: the ability to focus and change focus from near to far, to be able to see clearly as the eye moves along a line or up and down, to change focus easily, to make sense of small differences and likenesses and to have a visual memory. Children can be very good at hiding difficulties, their quiet coping strategies easily give the impression all is well.

Unlike the hearing impaired child, it may be that the introduction of visually interesting books, where the print dances across a patterned or coloured background, is the first time a child switches off from a book. The blurred, indistinct and muddled page is a headache rather than fun. The spacing of letters may make it difficult for a visually impaired child to understand where one word ends and another begins, 'The dragon rushed out of his cave' may become 'Thedragonrushedoutofhiscave' – off-putting for the best of readers! Letters which are clearly different when heard, may look very similar in print: for example, p,d,b; c,a,o; u,m,w. Confusion in understanding even simple words may result from a child's inability to actually see the differences.

Children who have a known visual difficulty or are suspected of having one should always be in good light: ceiling light alone may be insufficient and a reading or table lamp should be used as well at night. In daylight it is important to reduce glare from highly polished surfaces or shiny paper.

There are a large number of different kinds of type and of

'He drew a gun.' 'There was flour everywhere.' 'He rode on ahead.' Words can easily mislead!

Everyone has a right and a need to read.

type size. If type is very thick the space between words is automatically reduced which may make it harder for recognition. Lines which are very close together or which are particularly long can be a source of difficulty. Children who require special print or the use of specialist low vision aids should also receive advice and support from a qualified teacher of the visually impaired.

Learning to read is one of the most difficult tasks that *any* child undertakes. It becomes more problematic for a child with any additional difficulties, whether the disability is minor or major, temporary or permanent.

Reading involves many skills. It is often the case that 'reading problems' or 'failure' gives parents and teachers the first clue to the child's area of special need. Much of the work preceding reading will have been lost. Careful and thoughtful help can enable lost time to be made up. The necessary skills *can* be acquired despite persistent difficulties.

All children have a right to share in the fun of books, to enter the world of imagination, to have books which let them travel to any time and any place. Children who have special needs have just the same rights and need help and understanding to allow them to take advantage of the freedom books have to offer.

BOOKS FOR CHILDREN WITH SPECIAL NEEDS

Children may have short-term special needs – eg when coping with the loss of a parent – or special needs which are long-term – eg because of a permanent disability. The books in the following lists cover a variety of different needs and include books *for* children undergoing that experience, as well as books *about* special children which can be read by other children as well.

Books for older children with reading problems

By 'older' children, we mean quite a wide age range: from those seven-year-olds who are still at the beginning stages, through eight and nine-year-olds who are struggling, to ten and eleven-year-olds who are not yet fluent. The books in the following list have been chosen because their interest level is suitable for these older children, while being relatively simple. We have attempted to mention books suitable for each of these different ages and stages. Therefore, some will appeal more to the bottom end of this age range than the top, say, and some are easier than others. Look carefully at each title before making a final choice for your child, bearing in mind his level of ability and particular interests. A book he is really interested in will be easier to read!

Catching the child's interest is most important when reading is a difficult activity and books seem unpleasant, even frightening objects to be avoided, not explored. So funny books are often the answer: eg joke books, comic-strip books, cartoons, comics. Make him laugh and he might start to like reading!

If your child has a particular hobby or interest, try finding books about it. Information books are the way to reading for many children who are having difficulties. Although information books are often very demanding, it is surprising what children are able to read when they are interested and have some knowledge about the subject.

Don't forget, if a particular book seems a bit too difficult for your child, read it with him first, getting him to point to the words as you read together. If it still causes problems, then forget it for a while and try another book.

Picture books without words

Picture books without any words can be a good way back into books for older children who may have had early experiences of failure. They demonstrate that books can be a source of pleasure and get children into the habit of sitting and looking at a book for a concentrated period of time.

The following books can be enjoyed at different levels by any age, from 5 – 50 + !

Anno's Journey *Mitsumasa Anno*
    Bodley Head 1978 Hardback
Follow Anno on his journey through the ancient towns, villages and countryside of Europe and spot the stories and characters as you turn the pages: eg Red Riding Hood; Sesame Street characters; Beethoven sitting at a window etc. This book of soft, detailed pictures will appeal to any age.

The Great Green Mouse Disaster *Martin Waddell*
    Beaver 1989
A hamper-full of green mice escape in the foyer of a large, old hotel and cause havoc among staff and guests. Cut-away pictures of the inside of the hotel show many different stories that the reader can follow from page to page. With minutely detailed drawings to pore over for hours by Philippe Dupasquier.

The Great Escape *Philippe Dupasquier*
    Walker 1989
A prisoner escapes from gaol and a crazy chase ensues through the city, including a hospital, film studio, circus and into the country and back into gaol and . . .

Magical Changes *Graham Oakley*
    Picturemac 1987
A very imaginative picture book with split pages which create many fantastic images. (8 years + .)

Where's Wally?; Where's Wally Now?; Where's Wally? – The Forbidden Journey *Martin Hanford*
    Walker 1989
Three books in which you have to follow Wally on a journey and spot him on each crowded double page. Once looked, forever hooked. For Wally-watchers aged seven to seventy, but particularly suitable for children who are reluctant to read.

Books for older beginners

These range from very simple books for absolute beginners to those suitable for children who are beginning to make progress. These may be longer books with simple vocabulary, or picture books which will give visual clues to a short, but more difficult text.

A Bag Full Of Pups *Dick Gackenbach*
    Picture Puffin 1985
Mr Mullin finds homes for his 12 pups. (7–9 years.)

Brown Bear, Brown Bear, What Do You See? *Bill Martin, Jnr.*
    Picture Lion 1986
Very simple rhythmic, rhyming text showing different coloured animals. For absolute beginners.

Dr Seuss Books
    Collins 1960s
First published in the sixties, these books for beginners are still popular with all ages. Their zany nonsense makes them particularly suitable for children who do not enjoy reading. Special favourites include:

> For absolute beginners – **Bears In The Night** (already mentioned in more detail in Part 2); **Hop On Pop; Ten Apples Up On Top**.
> A little harder – **The Cat In The Hat; The Cat In The Hat Comes Back; Green Eggs And Ham; Fox In Socks**.
> And three joke books by Bennet Cerf:
> **Book Of Riddles; Book Of Animal Riddles; More Riddles**.

Going West *Martin Waddell*
    Picture Puffin 1985
A tough tale of settlers travelling west in a wagon train. The simple prose, superbly supplemented by Philippe Dupasquier's wide panoramas and pictures teeming with detail, tells of many hardships including the death of a child in the family but ends hopefully with a birth in the new home. (8 years + .)

The Great Big Enormous Turnip *Alexei Tolstoy*
    Piccolo 1972
The well-known, repetitive tale of pulling up the turnip, beautifully illustrated by Helen Oxenbury.

Have You Seen The Crocodile? *Colin West*
   Walker Reading Time 1990
A very simple text which repeats as it builds up. With
an amusing ending. (6–9 years.)

John Brown, Rose And The Midnight Cat *Jenny
Wagner*
   Picture Puffin 1979
A quiet, gentle tale of John Brown, the dog who feels
pushed out of his mistress's affections by the arrival of
the midnight cat, finely drawn by Ron Brooks.

**Little Dracula's Christmas; Little Dracula Goes To
School; Little Dracula's First Bite; Little Dracula
At The Seaside** *Martin Waddell*
   Walker 1987
The cartoon format and gory, slightly sick, sense of
humour are perfect for seven to eleven-year-olds.

Look What I've Got! *Anthony Browne*
   Magnet 1987
Stuck-up Jeremy has always got something better than
Sam. With lots of surrealistic details for observant
readers to spot.

A Country Far Away *Nigel Gray*
   Picture Puffin 1990
An original idea with pictures by Philippe Dupasquier.
The very different lives of two boys, one living in rural
Africa, one in the urban west, are shown in pictures
with one simple sentence per page. (8 years +.)

The Old Joke Book *Janet & Allan Ahlberg*
   Picture Puffin 1987
Full-colour comic strip format, speech bubbles and the
corniest jokes add up to a winning formula.

Owl At Home *Arnold Lobel*
   Heinemann I Can Read 1989
Five gently amusing short stories about Owl for readers
who are just beginning to get the idea of reading.

Up North In Winter *Deborah Hartley*
   MacDonald 1988
A reminiscence about Grandpa who found a dead fox
on the frozen lake. (7–11 years.)

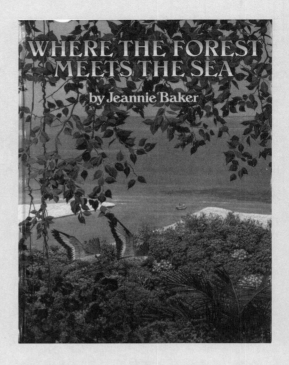

Where The Forest Meets The Sea *Jeannie Baker*
   Walker 1989
A stunning picture book with a conservationist theme.
A boy visits the tropical rain forest of Northern
Queensland. Amazing collage pictures. (7 years +.)

Willy The Wimp; Willy The Champ *Anthony Browne*
    Magnet 1986/7
Two stories in which inoffensive little Willy the chimp
gets the better of the streetwise gorilla gang and the
bully Buster Nose. Superb, witty drawings which will
appeal to the older beginner reader. (7–11 years.)

The following books, already mentioned in the 'Books
For Beginner Readers' section, also appeal to older
beginners. (See previous section for details.)

Bears In The Night *Stan & Jan Berenstain*
    Collins
Bet You Can't *Penny Dale*
    Walker Reading Time
Big Dog . . . Little Dog *P. D. Eastman*
    Picture Lion
Cat On The Mat Books *Brian Wildsmith et al*
    OUP
Funny Bones *Janet & Allan Ahlberg*
    Picture Lion
Happy Families *Allan Ahlberg & Colin McNaughton*
    Puffin
Frog And Toad Books *Arnold Lobel*
    Heinemann

Meg And Mog Books *Helen Nicoll & Jan Pienkowski*
    Picture Puffin
Monster And The Baby etc *Virginia Mueller*
    Picture Puffin
Red Nose Readers *Allan Ahlberg & Colin
McNaughton*
    Walker
Teeny Tiny *Jill Bennett*
    OUP

Books for older readers on the move

Children at this stage can be easily daunted
if there is too much text on a page, so it is
important that they still have picture books
as well as short novels with illustrations,
perhaps line drawings, to help them into
longer children's paperbacks.

Basil Brush Takes Off *Peter Firmin*
    Young Lion 1983
Basil and Harry the mole go to the beach. Basil and
Harry go animal hunting in India. Also: **Two Tales Of
Basil Brush**. (7–9 years.)

The Big Green Book *Robert Graves*
    Young Puffin 1978
Jack finds a book of magic spells in the attic. (8–10
years.)

Curtis The Hip-hop Cat *Gini Wade*
    Picturemac 1986
Curtis gains 'street cred' by learning to dance. A rap-
type rhyming story. (9 years +.)

**Dorrie And The Wizard's Spell; Dorrie And The
Birthday Eggs; Dorrie And The Haunted House;
Dorrie And The Goblin** *Patricia Coombs*
    Young Puffin 1982
Four books about this enchanting little witch, her cat,
Gink, and her mother, the Big Witch. (8–10 years.)

The Ha Ha Bonk Book *Janet & Allan Ahlberg*
   Puffin 1982
A great joke book with sections like 'Jokes to tell your teacher' and 'Jokes not to tell your teacher'.

Hiccup Harry *Chris Powling*
   Young Lion Jets 1988
Harry's hiccups cause havoc at school as he tries to cure them. Also: **Harry's Party**. (8–11 years.)

The Iron Man *Ted Hughes*
   Faber 1985
A gripping and imaginative fantasy, beautifully and clearly written. (10 years +.)

Jack At Sea *Philippe Dupasquier*
   Picture Puffin 1987
Adventures on board ship during the Napoleonic wars. Lots of historical detail in picture and text which is short but not easy.

The Jungle of Peril; The Planet Of Terror *Patrick Burston*
   Walker 1988
Two brilliantly illustrated adventure-game picture books with a challenge in every picture.

Mrs Simkin And The Magic Wheelbarrow *Linda Allen*
   Young Piper 1988
Two short stories about Mr and Mrs Simkin. (7–9 years.)

My Naughty Little Sister Goes Fishing *Dorothy Edwards*
   Magnet 1976
My naughty little sister is not allowed in the water but she still gets herself wet. This is one story from the collected stories, published as a picture book. Look out for other titles.

The following books, mentioned in more detail in previous sections, are also suitable for older children with reading difficulties:

Flat Stanley *Jeff Brown*
   Mammoth

Laura And The Bandits *Philippe Dumas*
   Young Lion

The Magic Finger *Roald Dahl*
   Young Puffin

The Shrinking Of Treehorn *Florence Parry Heide*
   Young Puffin

The Story Of Ferdinand *Munro Leaf*
   Young Puffin

Wildcat Wendy *Nancy Chambers*
   Fontana Lion

Books for children with disabilities

A to Z books *Beverley Matthias*
   Franklin Watts 1988 Hardback
Each book goes through the alphabet on a theme (**My Body; Animals; Food; Transport**) with a large coloured photograph for each letter of the alphabet. Each letter is finger-spelt at the top of the page and there is a simple sentence in print and in signed English. For hearing-impaired children.

Spot Books:
Where's Spot?; Spot Goes To School *Eric Hill*
   National Deaf Children's Society 1988
For hearing-impaired children. Sign language translation above each word.

Roly Goes Exploring *Philip Newth*
   Collins 1981
For blind and partially sighted children in braille and standard type, with shapes to find and feel.

Clear-Vision Books
   Linden Lodge School (in co-operation with RNIB), 61 Princes Way, London SW19 6JB
Picture books for loan, adapted for braille. Each page is interleaved with a transparent sheet with braille dots on it.

Large Print Books
   Lythway, Windsor Bridge Road, Bath BA2 3AX
Lythway publish a good range of full-length children's novels by top authors in big print for partially sighted children of 9 years +. Hardbacks priced around £7.50.

Books about children with disability

These books are equally important for able-bodied children, to make them more aware of what it might be like to have a disability. This list includes straightforward information books for younger children and novels for older children. The latter all deal positively with their subject, showing characters facing challenges with love, courage and determination.

Blue Boat *Dick Bruna*
 Methuen 1984
Hearing impairment. Pre-school.

Claire And Emma *Diana Peter*
 A. & C. Black 1976
With large, coloured photographs, it tells the story of two sisters, both born deaf. (4–7 years.)

Go Tell It To Mrs Golightly *Catherine Cookson*
 Corgi 1989
An adventure story with a blind girl as the central character.

Jessy Runs Away *Rachel Anderson*
 Young Lion Jets 1989
A Down's Syndrome child get lost. An easy read. (7–9 years.)

Let The Balloon Go *Ivan Southall*
 Puffin 1972
John has cerebral palsy and sets himself the challenge of climbing a tree. A gripping story of bravery and determination.

Mundo And The Weather Child *Joyce Dunbar*
 Piper 1987
Edmund loses his hearing when he is seven and enters a solitary world of the imagination. (9 years +.)

Peter Gets A Hearing Aid *Nigel Snell*
 Hamish Hamilton 1984
An informative little picture book for 5–7s.

Red Sky In The Morning *Elizabeth Laird*
 Piper 1989
About Anna's deep love for her profoundly disabled brother. (11 years +.)

Suzy *Elizabeth Chapman*
 Bodley Head 1982
A very simple information book, in big print and pictures, about Suzy who is partially sighted. (5–7 years.)

Warrior Scarlet *Rosemary Sutcliff*
 Puffin 1976
A Bronze Age boy must kill a wolf to prove his manhood but he has a withered arm. (9 years +.)

The Witch's Daughter *Nina Bawden*
 Puffin 1969
An adventure story in which the daughter's blindness is an advantage, making her other senses more acute. (8–10 years.)

Will The Real Gertrude Hollings Stand Up? *Sheila Greenwald*
 Puffin 1989
Gertrude is dyslexic. (As this book is American, she is referred to as 'Learning Disabled') (9 years +.)

Books for special situations

Dinosaurs Divorce (A Guide for Changing Families) *Laurene Krasny Brown & Marc Brown*
 Collins 1986 Hardback
Through pictures of little dinosaur characters, this book explains to young children the various aspects of divorce: eg trouble at home; having two homes; living with step-parents.

Going Into Hospital *Althea*
 Dinosaur 1986
An informative little book which explains to a young child in words and pictures what happens when you are in hospital.

Granpa *John Burningham*
　　Jonathan Cape 1989
John Burningham deals subtly with the problem of
death in this gentle story about a little girl and her
grandfather. (5–8 years.)

I Am Adopted *Susan Lapsley*
　　Bodley Head 1974
Delicate pictures. Sensitively handled for explaining to
a young child.

If You Meet A Stranger *Camilla Jessell*
　　Walker 1990 Hardback
A book for very young children with colour
photographs and simple information. Olu and her
playgroup are told by the policeman and policewoman
never to go with strangers. This is followed by an
incident in the park where Olu and her friend Paul
follow their advice.

I'll Always Love You *Hans Wilhelm*
　　Picture Knight 1986
A touching tale about a little boy coming to terms with
the death of his elderly and much-loved dog, Elfie. (4–7
years.)

Living With Mum *Jackie Stone*
　　Dinosaur 1989
Nicholas lives alone with his mother. Written in the
first person, he tells us about himself and his feelings.
(5–8 years.)

Mama's Going To Buy You a Mockingbird *Jean
Little*
　　Puffin 1985
The death of a father through cancer. A very moving
story. (9 years + .)

No More Secrets For Me *Oralee Wachter*
　　Puffin 1986
A collection of sensitively written stories about
children in sexually threatening situations. The
message is: 'Tell someone'. (7–11 years.)

The Pinballs *Betsy Byars*
　　Puffin 1980
Carlie is a disturbed and challenging youngster who
goes to a new foster home and does her best to create
trouble. She gradually comes to terms with her
situation through caring for Harvey and Thomas J,
also fostered. (10 years + .)

Susie And The Wise Hedgehog Go To Court *Madge
Bray*
　　Hawksmere 1989
Written by a social worker, this book is an attempt to
reassure children who will be giving evidence in court
by explaining how it works through the character, the
wise hedgehog. Beautiful illustrations carry the
plodding text.

There's A Sea In My Bedroom *Margaret Wild*
　　Picture Puffin 1989
David is afraid of the sea until magical things start to
happen when he takes a conch shell into his bedroom. A
stunning picturebook illustrated by Jane Tanner. (5–8
years.)

The Trouble With Donovan Croft *Bernard Ashley*
　　Puffin 1977
Donovan's mother has to go back to Jamaica and the
shock of being fostered causes him to stop speaking.

The Visitors Who Came To Stay *Annalena McAfee*
　　Hamish Hamilton 1987
Life changes for Katy when dad's girlfriend and her son
come to stay. Witty illustrations by Anthony Browne.
Picture story book to read with 7–9s.

Wheezy *Michael Charlton*
　　Bodley Head 1988 Hardback
William has asthma and makes it his project at school.

FURTHER READING AND USEFUL ADDRESSES

Learning To Read And Write *Wendy Body*
(Successful Parenting Guides) Longman 1989

I Need A Book! The Parent's Guide to Children's Books for Special Situations *Tony Bradman*
Thorsons Publishing Group 1987

Babies Need Books *Dorothy Butler*
Pelican 1988

See All, Say All – A selection of books for the language deprived child *Margaret K. Marshall*
For the British Section of IBBY (International Board of Books for Young People) 1985, available by post from Burchell and Martin Ltd. Tel: 021-643-18881

Helping Children Read, The Paired Reading Handbook *Roger Morgan*
Methuen 1986

From Birth To Five Years *Mary D. Sheridan*
NFER-Nelson 1975

The Read-Aloud Handbook *Jim Trelease*
Penguin Books 1984

Practical guides to making and doing

Favourite Dolls And Toys *Jean Greenhowe*
Hamlyn 1988
A hundred toys and dolls to sew and knit.

Make, Bake, Grow And Sew *Judy Hindley & Judy Bastyra*
Collins 1989

Toys For Kids *Sarah Stacey*
Elm Tree Books 1987
Simple soft toys to make.

Sing A Song Of Sixpence! *Jane Hart*
Gollancz 1983 (1988 paperback edition also available)
A book of songs suitable for 4 to 9-year-olds with accompaniment for piano or guitar.

Magazines about books, available on subscription

Books For Keeps
6 issues a year available from: 1 Effingham Road, Lee,
London SE12 8NZ

Books for Your Children
3 issues a year available from: 90 Gillhurst Road,
Harborne, Birmingham 17

Growing Point
6 issues a year available from: Ashton Manor,
Ashton, Northants NN7 2JL

Book Clubs selling books at a discount on published prices

Children's Book Club
BCA, Swindon X, SN99 9XX

Red House Books
Witney, Oxfordshire, OX8 6YQ
There are several other Book Clubs which you see advertised in magazines
and colour supplements.

Useful addresses

The Dyslexia Institute
133 Gresham Road, Staines, Middlesex TW18 2AJ

The British Dyslexia Association
98 London Road, Reading, Berks RG1 5AU

The Children's Book Foundation
Book Trust, 45 East Hill, London SW18 2QZ

The National Deaf Children's Society
45 Hereford Road, London W2 SAH
Telephone, Voice and Minicom: 071-229-9272/4

The National Library For The Handicapped Child
University of London Institute of Education, 20 Bedford Way,
London WC1H 0AL

The Royal National Institute For The Blind
224 Great Portland Street, London W1N 6AA

SOME TYPICAL QUESTIONS PARENTS ASK

Whenever we talk to parents about reading and language teaching there are certain areas of concern and questions which arise time and time again. The general ones like 'How can I best help my child to read?' or 'I'd like some advice about available books', and so on, are main themes of this book. Others are more specific and examples of common ones are listed in what follows. After each question you will find the main page references to answer the question, but do please bear in mind that some of the issues are addressed more generally in other places.

When should I start reading with my child?
Pages 18, 42–43

I'm not sure if my child's speech is about right for his age or if it is immature; how can I tell?
Page 23

How important is it for me to play with my very young baby?
Pages 26, 27

One school near us uses a reading scheme but my daughter's school doesn't. Is this all right?
Pages 57–60

What does 'phonics' mean?
Pages 61–62

I'm sure my child should be reading to the teacher every day, shouldn't he?
Pages 62–63

What's the best way of approaching my child's school about my concerns?
Pages 64–65

In a nutshell, what's the best support I can give my child at infant school?
Pages 65–66

How can I tell if a book is about right for my child or if it is too hard?
Page 67

How should I help my child when he can't read a word in his reading book? I'm always worried I'll do it wrong!
Pages 69–71

What's the best way to teach my child the alphabet?
Page 79

Does it matter what style of printing I teach my child to write?
Page 77

Are there any good ideas for teaching letter sounds at home?
Pages 79–80

What features in a book should I look at generally for my child who is beginning to read?
Page 82

My child reads quite well but doesn't really seem to be very interested in reading. What could I try?
Pages 90–92

I felt quite confident about helping my child with reading when he was in the infants but is there anything I should be doing now he's moved to the junior school?
Page 97

I think my eight-year-old daughter's reading is quite good but how can I be sure?
Pages 98–99

What IS the new National Curriculum?
Pages 55–57, 93–98

Help your Child with Reading

My child was very slow in starting to talk and he's been slow in reading too. How can I help him?
Pages 109–110, 115–118

My child sounds so boring *when he reads to me! How can I get him to read with more expression?*
Page 110

Are there any games we could play to help my child remember the words he finds difficult?
Page 111

I just can't seem to get my son to appreciate how important reading is. Any ideas?
Pages 111–112

We are considering arranging for extra private lessons to help my child's reading. What should we look out for?
Page 113

My husband and I have recently split up and now the children's school work seems to be affected. What can I do?
Pages 113–114

I think my child may be dyslexic – how can I find out? My child is dyslexic – what special help will be needed?
Pages 114–115

I've read something about Paired Reading being good for children with reading problems? What is it and can parents help?
Pages 115–117

My daughter's spelling is awful. Is there anything *I can do to help her?*
Pages 118–120

How will a slight hearing loss affect my child's reading?
Pages 121–124, 128–130

My little girl holds the book at a very funny angle when she is reading. Could this mean there is anything wrong with her eyesight?
Pages 126–128, 130–131

When/how should I teach the alphabet? Should I teach the names or sounds of the letters or both?
Pages 79–79

Is it really important to help my child with reading? Isn't that the school's job?
The answer to both these questions is yes. But it isn't simply an either/or situation! All parents want the best for their child and the best in reading terms comes about from the expertise of the school being supported by the special interest, involvement and care that parents are able to provide.

The path to literacy and the exploration of the world of books can be an exciting experience. Enjoy it with your child!

Index

ABC books, 50, 79
action rhymes, 18, 50–1
activities:
  for early learning, 24–42
  language development, 71–6
adoption, books to help with, 138
aloud, reading, 51–2, 100
alphabet:
  learning, 79
  see also letters
animal stories, 110
'Apprenticeship Approach' to
  reading, 58–9
assesssments:
  National Curriculum, 56, 93, 98
  reading progress, 98
asthma, 121
astigmatism, 126
Attainment Targets, National
  Curriculum, 56, 93

babies:
  activities and games, 24–42
  introducing books to, 19–20, 36,
    42–52
  learning to talk, 11–16
'ball and stick' style, writing, 77
ball games, 35
bedtime reading, 91–2
bedtime stories, 21, 114
Bingo, 111, 115
binocular-vision, 125
board books, 19, 44
book clubs, 140
book swaps, 90–1
books:
  access to, 90–1
  for beginner readers, 82–5
  books to read to your child, 86–
    7, 107
  books to read with your child,
    85–6
  for children with special needs,
    132–8
  child's own book, 75
  encouraging reading habit, 90–
    2
  first word books, 88
  introducing babies to, 19–20, 36,
    42–52
  and language development, 18–
    21
  learning to read in schools, 57–
    66
  listening to children read, 67–
    71
  for older readers, 100–7
  poetry, 88
  reading schemes, 57, 59–60, 129
  reasons for sharing, 11
boxes, playing with, 34–5
brain, and visual impairment,
  126
British Dyslexia Association,
  140
building games, 37–8

'can you see ...?' books, 52
capital letters, 77
cardboard books, 19, 44
catching games, 35
Children's Book Foundation,
  140
clapping songs, 32
classics, 105–6
clumsiness, 127
colour-blindness, 128
commands, learning to talk, 16
concentration span, 41
conductive hearing loss, 121–2
confidence, 16
consonants, and hearing loss,
  123
conversations, learning to talk,
  14–15
cookery, language development,
  73
coordination:
  hand/eye coordination, 30, 33,
    35, 39
  problems, 127
counting books, 49
Cripps, Charles, 118
cross-curricular approach, 94–5

deafness, 121–5
death, books to help with, 138
depth perception, 125
diabetes, 121
dictionaries, 88, 97, 118, 120
disabilities, special needs, 121–
  31, 136–7
diseases, and hearing loss, 122
divorce, books to help with, 137
dizziness, 128
doctors, 124, 125
double-vision, 125
Down's Syndrome, 121
dressing up, 41
dyslexia, 109, 114–15
Dyslexia Institute, 115, 140

ear, nose and throat specialists,
  124
ears, hearing loss, 121–5
educational psychologists, 115
emotional problems, 113–14
encyclopedias, 97
English language, National
  Curriculum, 55–7
expression, reading with, 110
eyes:
  eye contact, 13
  hand/eye coordination, 30, 33,
    35, 39
  visual impairment, 125–8, 130–1

fairy tales, 106, 110
fiction, 92–3, 97, 100–2
finger paints, 40–1
folk tales, 106, 110
friezes, alphabet, 79
frustration, hearing loss, 124

games:
  for early learning, 25–42
  language development, 71–6
  learning letter sounds, 79–81,
    111, 115
gestures, learning to talk, 15

'glue ear', 121
grapho-phonic information, 69
grommets, 121
group reading, 95–7

hand/eye coordination, 30, 33,
  35, 39
handling babies, 13
handwriting:
  forming letters, 77–8
  National Curriculum
    Attainment Target, 56
head injuries, and hearing loss,
  122
headaches, 128
Health Visitors, 124, 125, 126
hearing aids, 121, 122
hearing loss, 121–5
hospitals, books to help with, 137
hypermetropia, 126

I-spy, 52, 79
imagination, developing, 41
imitation, learning to talk, 15, 17
independence, young children,
  17
'Individualised Reading', 57–8,
  59, 60
information, 'reading for
  learning' skills, 95

jigsaws, 36–7, 39
junior schools, 92–9

language:
  games and activities to develop,
    71–6
  and hearing loss, 123–4
  language difficulties, 109–10
  learning to talk, 11–24
  listening skills, 129
  phonics, 61–2, 113, 129
  syntactic information, 69
learning:
  activities and games, 24–42
  to talk, 11–24
left-handed children,
  handwriting, 77
legends, 106
letter-writing, language
  development, 73–4
letters, 76–81
  alphabet, 79
  capitals, 77
  formation, 77–8
  sounds, 78–81
libraries, 71, 90, 95, 97
'lift-out' jigsaws, 39
linking words, 16
lipreading, 129
listening:
  listening skills, 128–9
  listening to children read, 67–
    71
  National Curriculum
    Attainment Target, 56
long sight, 126
'look-and-find' books, 19
Look, Cover, Write, Check
  method, spelling, 118–20
look-say method, 61

magazines, 112, 140
manipulative skills, 37, 38

matching shapes, 37, 39
meaning, 69, 129
memory:
  early learning games, 27
  visual, 118
middle ear problems, 121, 124
migraine, 121, 128
mobiles, 26, 36
monitoring progress, 98–9
monotonous reading, 110
motivation, 111–12
myopia, 125–6
myths, 106

names, language development, 72
National Curriculum, 55–7, 61, 70, 93, 98, 118
National Deaf Children's Society, 125, 140
National Library for the Handicapped Child, 140
newspapers, 112
non-fiction, 97
nonsense verse, 88
novels, 92–3, 97, 100–2
novelty books, 44–5
nursery rhymes, 18, 42, 50–1

Paired Reading, 115–17
paper, wrapping paper activities, 41–2
parents:
  activities and games for early learning, 26
  family reading time, 92
  liaison with school, 63–6
  listening to children read, 67–71
  monitoring reading progress, 99
  Paired Reading, 115–17
  parents' evenings, 98
  supporting junior school reading, 97
  typical questions, 141–2
pencils, holding, 77
Peters, Margaret, 118
phonics, 61–2, 113, 129
physical problems, 121–31, 136–7
  hearing loss, 121–5
  visual impairment, 125–8, 130–1
pictures, 35
  looking at illustrations, 68
  picture books, 19, 36, 45–6, 95, 133
  picture dictionaries, 88
play, early learning, 24–42
plays, 97
poetry, 88, 97, 106–7
prediction, in reading, 61
private lessons, 113
problem solving, 70
projects, cross-curricular approach, 94–5
pronouns, 16
pronunciation, learning to talk, 17
proof-reading, 118
psychiatrists, 115
psychologists, educational, 115
public libraries, 90, 97

questions, learning to talk, 16, 21–3

reading:
  books for beginners, 82–5
  books for older readers, 100–7
  books to read to your child, 86–7, 107
  books to read with your child, 85–6
  cross-curricular approach, 94–5
  encouraging reading habit, 90–2
  in junior schools, 92–9
  listening to children, 67–71
  monitoring progress, 98–9
  motivation, 111–12
  National Curriculum, 56–7, 61, 93
  Paired Reading, 115–17
  poetry, 88, 97, 106–7
  private lessons, 113
  reading aloud, 51–2, 100
  reading time in school, 62–3
  school/parent liaison, 63–6
  in schools, 55–66
  special needs, 108–38
  stamina, 95, 102–3
  unfamiliar words, 69–71
  'reading for learning' skills, 95
reading games, 79–81, 111, 115
reading schemes, 57, 59–60, 129
'Real Books, approach to reading, 58, 59
reference books, 95, 97
reluctant readers, 111–12
rhymes:
  listening skills, 129
  nursery rhymes, 18, 42, 50–1
  poetry, 88
Royal National Institute for the Blind (RNIB), 126, 140

schemes, reading, 57, 59–60, 129
schools:
  bookshops, 90
  learning to read in, 55–66
  liaison with parents, 63–6
  monitoring reading progress, 98
  reading in junior schools, 92–9
  reading time, 62–3
scrapbooks, 112
semantic information, 69
sentences, learning to talk, 16–17
shape matching, 37, 39
sharing books, 11, 46–9, 55, 66, 67–71, 85–6
short sight, 125–6
singing games, 32
smell, early learning, 27
sorting games, 38
sounds:
  acquiring sounds in speech, 23
  early learning, 26–7
  grapho-phonic information, 69
  hearing loss, 122
  letters, 78–81
  listening skills, 128–9
  phonics, 61–2, 113, 129
speaking, National Curriculum

Attainment Target, 56
special needs, 108–38
'specific learning difficulty' *see* dyslexia
speech:
  acquiring sounds, 23
  and hearing loss, 123–4
  learning, 11–24
  speech therapy, 23
spelling, National Curriculum Attainment Target, 56
spelling problems, 118–20
squints, 125
stamina, reading, 95, 102–3
Standard Assessment Tasks (SATs), 98
stories, 18
  bedtime stories, 21, 114
  fiction, 92–3, 97, 100–2
stress, 113–14
syntactic information, 69

talking:
  acquiring sounds, 23
  learning, 11–24
tape recorders, 110
taste, early learning, 27
teachers:
  assessing reading progress, 98
  dyslexic children, 115
  liaison with parents, 63–6
  private lessons, 113
  reading schemes, 59–60
  reading to, 62–3
  see also schools
television, and language development, 18
temper tantrums, 124
tests and assessments:
  hearing, 122
  National Curriculum, 56, 93, 98
  reading progress, 98
  visual, 125
thesauruses, 97
tinnitus, 128
topics, cross-curricular approach, 94–5
touching, 13–14, 27
toys, early learning, 26

unfamiliar words, 69–71

videos, and language development, 18
visual impairment, 125–8, 130–1
visual memory, 118
vocabulary, 118
vowel sounds, and hearing loss, 123

words:
  first word books, 88
  learning to read, 55
  look–say method, 61
  phonics, 61–2
  unfamiliar, 69–71
wrapping paper activities, 41–2
writing:
  cross-curricular approach, 94–5
  forming letters, 77–8
  National Curriculum Attainment Target, 56
  spelling problems, 118–20